TRACK
AND SIGN

A GUIDE TO THE FIELD SIGNS OF MAMMALS AND BIRDS OF THE UK

JOHN RHYDER

The
History
Press

TRACK AND SIGN

First published 2021

The History Press
97 St George's Place, Cheltenham,
Gloucestershire, GL50 3QB
www.thehistorypress.co.uk

British Library Cataloguing in Publication Data.
A catalogue record for this book is available from the British Library.

ISBN 978 0 7509 9614 3

Typesetting and origination by The History Press
Printed in Turkey by Imak

CONTENTS

PART 1 TRACKS

PART 2 SIGN

FOREWORD

Time in the field with John Rhyder always inspires me. We have a habit of looking at different things, but this is what is so enjoyable. John's observations remind me how much more there always is to discover.

Outdoor specialists learn certain instincts. We learn to spot the signs within our field without hesitation. In my area of natural navigation, I recognise the key shapes and patterns within trees, constellations and clouds, for example. After many years, these observations become automatic.

This approach works in all other fields too. The patterns vary, but experience makes them leap out and it's always a joy to witness. John sees the movement of a deer in the angle of leaves – he can't help it.

There is another instinct that experts develop – a sense for those who are born to share these skills. It is so exciting when someone pushes their knowledge to the point where their expertise becomes an art form. But teaching is not the same as doing; experts only make good authors if they keep sight of the path they followed.

There are some who profess a mysterious ability that can't be explained. These aren't the best people to learn from. Expertise is a journey that starts by spotting the same simple patterns, repeatedly. Great teachers don't claim strange powers, they show you the patterns. John does not claim a mystical provenance for his skills. He explains how he gained his insights and values the work of others, especially the CyberTracker approach. But he has gone on to develop these skills in his own way.

This is what makes John's work so refreshing and valuable; he shares his extensive experience, but never abandons the path he followed. He shows us the patterns that are worth looking for and invents none. It is a rare approach, one that teaches us how to see what is really there.

Tristan Gooley

PHOTO CREDITS

I have had a good deal of support from the tracking community in Europe to compile the images for this book. I have credited these contributors by using their initials after each image, as can be seen below. Any images not highlighted in this way, together with all the line drawings, are the work of the author.

In alphabetical order:

BO	Beke Olbers
BM	Brian McConnell
CP	Cris Palmares
DP	Dan Puplett
DC	Dave Crosbie
DM	David Moskowitz
DW	David Wege
GH	Graham Hunt
IM	Immo Meyer
JK	Jörn Kaufhold
KC	Kim Cabrera
LE	Lea Eyre
MB	Matt Binstead
RH	Rebecca Hosking
RN	Rene Nauta
RA	Richard Andrews
RB	Rob Brumfitt
SM	Sally Mitchell
SR	Simone Roters
TB	Thomas Baffault

ACKNOWLEDGEMENTS

In addition to everyone mentioned above who donated photographs allowing the completion of this work, I would especially like to thank the CyberTracker community of evaluators in North America, who have tracked, trained and worked with me to make me a better tracker and naturalist. In no particular order, they are Nate Harvey, Brian McConnel, Marl Elbroch, Casey Mcfarland, David Moskowitz and George Leoniak.

I would especially like to thank the British Wildlife Centre for allowing me access to their animals and David Wege for reading through this before I embarrassed myself too much and sent it to the publishers. Thanks to Louis Liebenberg for the whole concept of CyberTracker and creating such an excellent educational tool.

Thanks, as always, goes to my family for their continued help and support.

A final thank you to this wonderful world and its wildlife that continues to be so fascinating.

ABOUT THE AUTHOR

John Rhyder is a naturalist, wildlife tracker and woodsman and is certified through CyberTracker Conservation as a Senior Tracker. This involves being evaluated and scoring 100 per cent at Specialist level in both track and sign identification and trailing or following the animal. He is the first person in Northern Europe to become a Senior Tracker. John is also an evaluator for the CyberTracker assessment system.

He is fascinated by the natural world and the skills and knowledge that support our interaction with it. John writes and teaches about natural history, wildlife, tracking, ethnobotany and bushcraft.

INTRODUCTION

Track and Sign covers the main sign left behind by mammals – at least those that don't fly – and those birds that commonly leave tracks. I have included lots of illustrations but have limited any explanations to those that specifically explain the track and sign and why it might be there.

Understanding animal behaviour is a crucial part of becoming a great tracker, but the status and distribution of wildlife and a myriad of other details lie outside the scope of this book. I have also included track and sign of reptiles and amphibians and some insects, especially where these are commonly encountered. Both of these subjects could form tracking studies in their own right and so I talk about their tracks in very general terms. However, if a tracker stares at the ground for long enough they will come across this sign, so a ballpark idea of what it might be will be useful.

Much of the subject matter of this work is, I hope, fairly new and not widely known. It has stemmed from my involvement in the world of CyberTracker, and discovering the level of detail it is possible to pull from tracks on the landscape since meeting up with some remarkable trackers involved in this system.

I have set out the sections on sign in what I believe to be a logical fashion to aid the tracker in the field. As such, they are variously titled scats, damage to fungi, trees and plants, digs and scrapes, etc. This as opposed to listing every piece of sign left by each individual species, so hopefully the tracker can jump straight to the relevant section and start looking.

Tracks are explained in detail and each has a photo or several photos. I have tried to include, where possible, both the perfect track and examples of ones that are more frequently encountered, those that may be a bit smeared or incomplete. The tracks are arranged in family groups which have similar features.

There is a companion volume to this book which just contains the track drawings and can also be taken out into the field independently. It is designed to be laid alongside a track for a direct comparison and hopefully identification.

In addition to wild animals, I have also included the main domestic species found in our landscape. It is not unusual to encounter the tracks of alpaca in the woods as people organise walks with these creatures. Equally, it is not unusual to come across the sign of cattle and ponies in remote locations as the process of ecosystem restoration becomes more widespread. There are one or two exotics included, which may or may not establish in our landscape in the future.

John Rhyder, March 2020
www.woodcraftschool.co.uk

WHAT IS TRACKING?

According to the great South African tracker Louis Liebenberg, tracking may well be the origin of scientific thought and methodology. The premise for Louis's theory is that in order to track an animal to the extent that one may find it, one must first hypothesise as to where the animal is likely to be, and then use the tracks and sign to confirm that the animal's whereabouts are as first suspected. Should further evidence from the track and sign indicate that the tracker's original idea was wrong, then a new hypothesis must be formed using this new information gathered from the actual process of tracking that animal. In short, the tracker imagines or hypothesises where the animal might be found and uses the tracks to either prove or disprove this theory.

Tracking an animal therefore becomes a two-stage process. Firstly, identification of track and sign; and secondly, using those tracks and sign in conjunction with a sound theory to follow and find the animal. This second stage in the process is trailing. These two aspects of the subject can be treated separately, and indeed many trackers become proficient at only track and sign identification, even to a professional level. They may or may not explore the possibilities that trailing has to offer. The two aspects are two sides of the same coin and work hand in hand with each other, although this book deals exclusively with track and sign.

THE CYBERTRACKER SYSTEM

As an advocate of traditional ecological knowledge, Louis Liebenberg was very aware of the loss of knowledge from indigenous peoples across his native Africa. In tracking, Louis saw a perfect application for the astounding natural history knowledge many of these people still possessed, using it for wildlife survey and monitoring. With this in mind, he developed an icon-driven data capturing program. This meant that regardless of the user's level of literacy, local people could enter the Bush, find wildlife track and sign, tap the icon corresponding with that species, and then have all that data automatically uploaded onto a GPS. This is the 'cyber' element of the CyberTracker system.

The reliability of using this system, however, can be undermined should the person gathering the information not be a reliable tracker. To combat this, Louis developed an evaluation process to objectively test observer reliability. The resulting CyberTracker evaluation system is split into two distinct areas: Track & Sign, and Trailing, each of which is further divided into Standard- and Specialist-level evaluations that are scored as follows.

TRACK AND SIGN EVALUATION

TRACK & SIGN I
The candidate must be able to interpret the track and sign of medium to large animals and must have a fair knowledge of animal behaviour. To qualify for the Track & Sign Level I certificate, the candidate must obtain 69 per cent on the Track & Sign Interpretation evaluation.

TRACK & SIGN II
The candidate must be able to interpret the track and sign of small to large animals, interpret less distinct sign, and must have a good knowledge of animal behaviour. To qualify for the Track & Sign II certificate, the candidate must obtain 80 per cent on the Track & Sign Interpretation evaluation.

TRACK & SIGN III AND IV
The candidate must be able to interpret the track and sign of any animal, interpret obscure sign, and must have a very good knowledge of animal behaviour. To qualify for the Track & Sign III certificate, the candidate must obtain 90 per cent on the Track & Sign Interpretation evaluation, and for Level IV, 100 per cent.

TRACK & SIGN SPECIALIST CERTIFICATE

The candidate must be able to interpret the track and sign of any animal, interpret very obscure sign, and must have an excellent knowledge of animal behaviour. To qualify for the Track & Sign Specialist certificate, the candidate must obtain 100 per cent on a Track & Sign Interpretation Specialist evaluation.

TRACK & SIGN SPECIALIST EVALUATION

The process during the Track & Sign Specialist evaluation is identical to the above-described evaluations, except for the following variation. At least fifty very difficult Track & Sign questions will be asked, along with no more than ten difficult questions. No easy Track & Sign questions will be asked. In addition to this, seven extremely difficult Track & Sign questions will be asked.

No penalty is awarded for an incorrect answer on an extremely difficult question, but three correctly answered extremely difficult Track & Sign questions cancel the mistake of one incorrect answer. Thus, participants can rectify up to two mistakes during an evaluation and still earn their Specialist certificates.

TRAILING EVALUATION

TRAILING I

The candidate must be a fair, systematic tracker and be able to track humans or large animals. He or she must have a fair ability to judge the age of sign. To qualify for the Trailing I certificate, the candidate must obtain 70 per cent on the trailing of a human or large mammal spoor.

TRAILING II

The candidate must be a good, systematic tracker and be able to track large animals. He or she must have a fair ability to judge the age of sign. To qualify for the Trailing II certificate, the candidate must obtain 80 per cent on the trailing of a large mammal.

TRAILING III AND IV

The candidate must be a good, systematic tracker and be able to track medium or large animals. He or she must have a fair ability to judge the age of spoor. To qualify for the Trailing III certificate, the candidate must obtain 90 per cent on the trailing of medium or large mammal spoor. To qualify for the Trailing IV certificate, the candidate must obtain 100 per cent on the trailing of a medium or large mammal.

TRAILING SPECIALIST CERTIFICATE

The Trailing Specialist evaluation is done in varying (easy, difficult and very difficult) terrain on an animal that is difficult to follow, and must be conducted by both an evaluator and an external evaluator.

The candidate must be a good, speculative tracker. This includes the ability to predict where spoor will be found beyond the vicinity directly ahead of the tracker. He or she must be good at judging the age of spoor and must be able to detect signs of stress, or the location of carcasses from spoor. The Trailing Specialist must obtain 100 per cent on the trailing of a difficult animal trail.

CYBERTRACKER IN THE NORTHERN HEMISPHERE

The CyberTracker system rapidly grew in popularity across southern Africa and soon came to the attention of Mark Elbroch, an American tracker, author, biologist and mountain lion researcher. Mark travelled to Africa to learn the system directly from Louis, and together they brought it to America.

It wasn't long before Mark's work became known in Europe, and Mark was approached to come to the UK to establish the system here and in the rest of northern Europe. The first evaluations in our region were held in 2012 in West Sussex, hosted by me. On these evaluations were two other trackers, soon to become important figures in European wildlife tracking: René Nauta, of The Netherlands, and Joscha Grolms, from Germany, both of whom, together with myself, are now evaluators in the CyberTracker system.

Together with our American colleagues, the three of us have worked hard at finding the same standard and level of detail in tracking and trailing information that is available in South Africa and North America. Inspired by the level of detail we were shown by our American colleagues, and immediately after the first evaluation in the UK, we realised there could be much more detail in the information and literature available to European trackers. With this in mind, I began to run captive animals across ink and other substrates to separate some of our more closely related species and to pull as much detail from the tracks as possible.

Following on from this, Joscha and René have also conducted their own research using similar methods. So much so that we are now confident that this, and the work of René and Joscha, offer something significant and new to European tracking.

While North American trackers were instrumental in establishing CyberTracker in northern Europe, trackers from Africa were working with some excellent people in the south of our continent, most notably José Galán of Spain, also a CyberTracker evaluator. It is therefore now possible to explore and use CyberTracker standards across the whole of Europe.

USES OF TRACKING AND TRAILING

It is fair to say that tracking is underused in our region of the world. It has become the preserve of enthusiastic amateurs and is not always given the general credibility it deserves as a serious tool for the field naturalist. While track and sign may not entirely replace modern techniques of wildlife monitoring, it can certainly augment them, and may in some instances be superior.

Consider the amount of ground a trained tracker can cover versus the number of camera traps that may have to be deployed to get the same kind of coverage. When looking at it in this way, it is clearly cost-effective to train trackers to a high standard to ensure observer reliability.

This makes tracking an ideal, if not necessary, tool in the armoury of today's competent field naturalist. It is especially useful in detecting the presence or absence of unusual or difficult to observe species. It can also be used to estimate population densities. Furthermore, track and sign can establish the location of regularly used travel routes, which, in turn, may inform the placement of such things as badger gates and underpasses when considering new road and rail developments.

Coupled with modern techniques such as GPS collars or camera traps, more information can be gathered than by simply using the technology alone. Recently, I had the pleasure to accompany Mark Elbroch and his team in Washington State, USA, as they visited mountain lion GPS clusters. These are indications given off by the radio-collared mountain lions in Mark's study group.

The cluster refers to multiple GPS signals that have been fairly static or 'clustered' around a location for a time period of perhaps a day or two. Usually, this would indicate that the animals have made a kill and have been feeding.

Using telemetry, the kill site can be homed in on, and then the various mountain lion trails coming and going can be followed using tracking skills to gather extra information. This includes information on the kill itself, its status and the species preyed upon. It can also show what else has been feeding there. Trails may lead to latrine sites, allowing the possibility of DNA sampling and, as not all the animals are likely to be collared, this approach to surveying can indicate the number of individuals around the kill site.

In conjunction with technology, tracking may also inform the tracker as to the best possible place to aim trail cameras to increase the chance of catching the target on film.

In the UK, specialist knowledge of the tracks of protected species, and those species likely to be confused with them, is a must for any ecologist working in this field. In the world of forestry, deer numbers are at a level possibly greater than at any time in our history. Recognition of deer sign and the ability to separate sign of the various species and then to separate that sign from any other animal can only add to the effectiveness of programmes designed to control deer damage.

Recreationally, tracking is a wonderful skill to learn for the amateur naturalist, enhancing any walk in the countryside. For the photographer, it can put you in just the right spot for that winning image, and as with many of

The author's view from a mountain lion bed in Washington State, USA.

forms of nature connection, tracking can effectively enhance wellbeing. Tracking can also be used in tackling wildlife crime and assisting in search and rescue.

As a fundamental part of who we are as human beings, it touches something deep within the psyche. In all the things I have done in my outdoor career, never have I felt so connected to the natural world than when trailing. When I track well, it becomes intensely absorbing in the same way as I hear people describe flow states and mindfulness. In these moments, the trail reveals itself, stretching into the distance. The direction of the wind is noted almost subconsciously, the alarm calls of birds are obvious and the track and sign of all the other animals, even insects, crossing your trail reveal themselves. It's a strangely peaceful state where every sense seems to be stretched to the limit in a state of extreme concentration, and yet one feels completely relaxed and at peace. The whole of nature is revealed within an animal trail.

PART I

TRACKS

MAMMAL TRACKS

FOOT MORPHOLOGY

Eons ago, all that existed mammal-wise was a primitive, five-toed shrew-like creature from which all mammals have descended. This creature had hands and feet arranged in a way that differed very little to the present day. This arrangement is typically five toes on both front and rear feet, with toe pads to protect the delicate tips of the toe bones, palm pads to protect the joints at the other end of these delicate bones and, in the case of the front feet, carpal pads to protect the bones of the wrist. Within this group, especially with the smaller animals, the palm pads are often separate, forming individual cushions. The toes are numbered one to five, counting from the inside, with toe number one being the equivalent of the human thumb on the front, or big toe on the rear. The lagomorphs – rabbits and hares – don't have pads as such, but instead their delicate bones are protected by a mat of stiff fur. In these tracks, often only the claws will show.

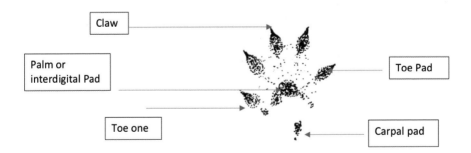

The front right track of a mink, a plantigrade animal. Note how the palm pads are separate cushions. The toes are numbered one to five starting from the inside of the equivalent of our thumb.

The original shrew-like mammals walked in a flat-footed fashion, with most of the sole of the foot capable of making contact with the ground. These sole-walkers, or plantigrade animals, are still with us today, and in the UK include the following groups: insectivores; mustelids; rodents; lagomorphs; and primates including us humans.

Some species of plantigrades still have five toes on the front foot and five on the rear. In particular, the mustelids and insectivores (and humans). Some, however, the rodents and lagomorphs (rabbits and hares), have lost one of the toes. In the case of rodents, many have lost the thumb (toe number one) on the front foot, and the lagomorphs have lost the big toe on the rear foot. However, there may be a vestigial impression of the thumb in the front track of some rodents, but it's so insignificant we can largely ignore it for identification purposes. Even in the species that still have five toes present on their front feet, the thumb often doesn't show well, or indeed at all, in the track.

Walking flat-footed is a relatively slow form of locomotion, although some plantigrade animals can really move if they have to. Just imagine trying to outrun a charging (plantigrade) brown bear!

Above left: Look closely at the bottom left track of this set of four. The vestigial toe one of this grey squirrel is just visible on the edge of the inside carpal pad.

Above middle: The vestigial toe can be seen in the (right front) foot of this grey squirrel.

Above right: Separate pads are visible on the rear foot of this yellow-necked mouse.

The next foot type belongs to the groups of animals moving primarily on the tips of their digits. These we called digitigrades, or finger walkers to keep it simple. Their feet are arranged with toe pads protecting the ends of the finger bones, and palm pads protecting the toe joints at the other end of these, but in contrast to the plantigrades these pads are fused together into one large structure.

The carpal pad can still be found on the front foot of digitigrades, but because these animals are up on their toes, this pad is now high up the leg. It will show in the track only if the substrate is very deep and occasionally if the animal jumps from a height.

Note how the carpal pad shows on this cat track, the animal having jumped down from a height. You can also see a hint of some of the claws.

In our region we have feline, canine and vulpine animals representing the digitigrades. These species generally have five toes on the front foot and four on the rear, but toe number one on the front track is represented by the dew claw, which will only register in deep substrate or if the animal is moving really fast. Some breeds of domestic animals show five toes in both their front and rear tracks.

Often the tracks of digitigrades register most deeply with the toes, and less so with the palm pad. Essentially, these animals have tilted forwards onto their toes for speed, and when they move flat out on hard ground the tracks may not show palm pads at all.

The blunt claws of canines are there for digging but may also be used for increased traction, just like running spikes. At high speeds, and on some substrates, only the claws of dogs may show.

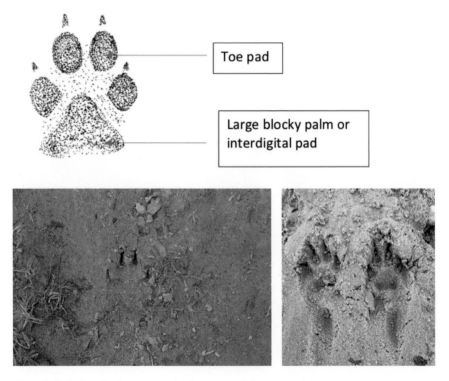

Toe pad

Large blocky palm or interdigital pad

Above left: On hard substrates, only the claws of dogs may show.

Above right: This dog came to a sudden stop, revealing its carpal pads and dew claws.

The final mammal foot type is found in the unguligrades, or ungulates, that have a toe pad equivalent to our own fingertip, but with a vastly modified nail (or hoof) which they are effectively walking on. We can call them nail-walkers or cloven-footed animals.

With the exception of the horse, all the representatives of this group in our region are walking on the nails of toes three and four. Horses walk on the end of toe three, although there has been some fusion of other digits over the eons and so it's not quite as simple as this. In some other countries there are more odd-toed ungulates than we have, for example rhinos have three toes on each foot.

Aside from horses and their like, our ungulate fauna comprises cows, sheep, goats, pigs and wild boar, and six species of deer (seven including reindeer). Also, increasingly regular in our landscape are more exotic creatures such as alpaca.

All of these species have lost toe one altogether, in terms of it registering in the track. Toes two and five are much reduced in size and higher up the leg and, as with dogs and cats, are referred to as dew claws. These may register reliably in the track in the case of pigs, or only in deep substrate or at high speeds in the case of deer.

The toe pads of ungulates register in their tracks with differing regularity between species, to the extent that its presence, size and shape can be diagnostic in identification. The underside of the modified nail (the hoof) is hollow and called the subunguis. The hoof wall, or unguis, is a major component of the track itself, forming much of the detail and shape produced on the ground, and frequently the deepest part of the track. These animals are called ungulates because they walk on their unguis.

These evolutionary adaptations are largely accepted as being driven by speed: plantigrades being relatively slow moving compared with animals that stand on their toes, which, in turn, are slower than animals that are now high up on their nails.

subunguis

Hoof wall

Toe pad

This goat track shows the elements of an ungulate track most commonly encountered.

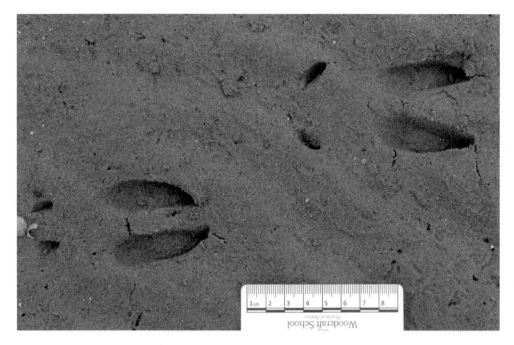

These are the rear and front tracks of a roe deer. It was moving reasonably quickly over soft substrate and so the dew claws (toes two and five) are showing. Note the angle and position of these relative to the rest of the track to identify front and rear.

NB: there are several photographs of various animal feet further along in this book.

WHAT TO LOOK FOR IN A TRACK

There are several components of a track that should be considered when trying to get to grips with smudges and holes in the mud and discerning their ownership. The process outlined here will become subconscious after a while as you build up more experience. Just as you can probably look at a cow and say immediately, 'That's a cow', and probably just as easily see a leg, an udder or an ear and still be fairly happy it's a cow, you will develop this 'one-glance' skill with tracks if you persevere.

This 'fast-thinking' approach will make you a much better or, should I say, more effective tracker. For more information on fast thinking, read Tristan Gooley's (2018) book *Wild Signs and Star Paths*.

Finding clear tracks with all the toes, nails and pads showing as they should do is the exception rather than the norm. Frequently, all a tracker has in front of them is a seemingly smudged mess, a partial track, or a track that has been distorted by the weather – which is just as well as I would be out of a job if it were too simple! I hope this book and its explanations will do something to unravel the mysteries of such imperfect tracks.

CONTEXT

When tracking, it's always a good idea to look at the context in which a particular track is found, including the region and habitat you are in. Even before you venture out it's a good idea to get to know what lives there. While it's not impossible that you have found evidence of a rarity, generally you are much more likely to find tracks and sign of the commonly occurring animals in your region.

However, many mammals are shy and elusive, and tracking can be a powerful tool in establishing the presence of an unusual or rare creature. I myself found tracks of otters on my local river, establishing the presence of this species as they made a comeback in West Sussex. These tracks also gave me the best location for a trail camera, which then captured images of a lactating otter indicating that not only were otters back, but they were also breeding.

SIZE VERSUS MORPHOLOGY

The size of a track is not as important, in my opinion, as its general morphology. I very rarely, if ever, measure tracks to aid identification, at least not exactly. I might think, 'That's way too big for a fox', for example, but I won't generally measure it. A big fox track is the same in appearance as a medium-sized fox track and a baby fox track.

I think far too much emphasis can be placed on size rather than the characteristics and morphology of the track. The emphasis on measuring tracks rather than careful examination of morphology explains the multitude of big dog track pictures I get sent to confirm the presence of 'big cats' in the UK. However, bird tracks are generally much more consistent size-wise, and so size can be used with greater effect to aid their identification.

SYMMETRY

Imagine a line drawn down through the middle of the track and check for symmetry. If both sides look fairly equal it rules out a large number of our mammals. With animals that have five toes, even if toe number one is hard to see, the track will often look asymmetrical. Sometimes the missing thumb (toe number one) is revealed by the shape of an asymmetrical palm pad. This pad will still be in place to protect the jointed end of the delicate finger bone and indicate where the thumb should be. Cats, although only having four toes, often leave a track that is asymmetrical. This is especially the case with the front track, which frequently shows three evenly spaced toes and then one sticking out all on its own.

TOES

The shape and size of toes is a crucial consideration in track identification. By size, I mean estimated size relative to the whole track, and not, as already discussed, by measuring with a ruler. Toes may be small in relation to the palm pads and/or claws, and the arrangement of toes around the palm pads is also important to note.

Ask yourself if all or most of the toes are arranged around the pad, or do they sit ahead of it? If they are a long way ahead of the palm pad, this may indicate an animal with long fingers, like a squirrel.

Toes may be bulbous, round, oval and or even triangular in shape.

PALM PADS

Check carefully the shape and relative size of the palm pads. These may be fused or made up of many individual pads. Palm pads may be lobed, symmetrical, almost symmetrical or highly asymmetrical. Be aware that some of the subtler features on palm pads may distort to the point that they disappear, which is especially true of lobes.

CLAWS

Claws are perhaps the least reliable feature when trying to positively identify a track. In some animals, where they are supposed to be present, frequently they won't show. Conversely, in some animals where they aren't supposed to show, they frequently do.

When claws do show, it is good practice to break down the relative size and shape based on how animals use their feet. If the animal predominantly runs, then the claws are likely to be fairly robust and this will show in the tracks they leave. If the animal regularly climbs or digs then its claws will look completely different, and if an animal uses claws to hold prey, they will be different again.

NEGATIVE SPACE

Most tracks show areas of 'negative space', which are the parts of the track that aren't made by the toes or the pads. Negative space is where the substrate still distorts to a greater or lesser degree or forms a vague compression shape between the toes or pads. It may form a distinctively shaped, raised ridge of mud squished between the toes or pads and, in the case of many animals, this can be especially helpful with track identification. It may also be the absence of obvious detail in species such as rabbits and hares whose furry feet can create mere 'shadows' on the ground.

SHAPE AND SIZE DIFFERENCES BETWEEN FRONT AND REAR

If you have a full set of tracks, or at least a front and rear track, useful comparative information can be gleaned. Many animals have different-sized front and rear feet, depending on where their weight is distributed. Some species may show a considerable difference in this regard, especially between the sexes. For example, the males of heavy-antlered deer species often show a very large front track in comparison to the rear. This is an adaptation to support not only the head and shoulders, but also the added weight of the antlers.

The rear tracks of many mammals with even-length legs are smaller and slimmer than the fronts, which are often as wide as they are long, or close to it. Learning to identify front and rear tracks is essential when trying to determine how an animal is moving, as described later in the section on gaits.

WHICH SIDE OF THE BODY?

It is often possible to work out which side of the body a track comes from as well as whether it is a front or rear foot. Together with any obvious size difference, there are a couple of other features to think about. With digitigrade animals, the longest toe, just like our own hand, is toe number three. This leading toe will therefore always be on the inside of the track, closest to the body. Conversely, deer species frequently show toe four as the longest. In the track, this means that if there is a difference, the shortest toe will be on the inside. It is also worth looking at the palm pads in tracks, as these may narrow or angle down towards the centre of the trail.

SEX

It can be difficult to sex animals from their tracks, unless of course there is an obvious size difference as alluded to above. Sometimes other factors may help us determine the sex if a set of tracks is found. For example, the position of urine in relation to rear tracks may help, as would the presence of smaller tracks from younger animals following the tracks you are studying. Also, groups of evenly sized animals will suggest same-sex groups moving through the landscape together. In some species, notably the mustelids, there is a big difference between the physical size of the males compared to the females, and this transfers to the track size.

MEASURING TRACKS

Despite my earlier comments about the exact sizes of tracks being of limited use for identification, I have included average track measurements in this book. The illustrations represent average-sized tracks that I have found on my travels, and they are printed life-sized. The measurements are of these tracks, and they are measured from the tip of the longest toe to the end of the furthest, regularly present pad in the case of soft-footed animals. In the case of hoofed animals, the measurement is from the tip of the longest cleat, if there is a difference, to the end of the toe pad if it shows in the track. Width is measured from the widest point on both sides.

My hope is that you can do a direct comparison of the illustrations, plus or minus a few per cent in terms of size, and match them based on morphology. This may be easier with the companion *Animal Tracks Field Guide* which has been published to accompany this work. Do keep in mind that there is always the possibility of exceptional-sized examples of some of these animals and their tracks.

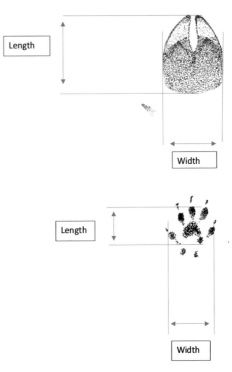

The measurements I have given do not include carpal pads or ungulate dew claws as, even with animals that have them, they frequently do not show in the track.

The wild boar track on the previous page serves to illustrate how I have measured tracks for this book. Note that even though dew claws show reliably with this species they are not included in the measurements.

Below the boar track is the front right foot of a hedgehog, neither claws nor carpal pads are included in the measurements.

HOW TO INTERPRET TRACKS

It may seem like common sense but, as mentioned above, tracks need to be viewed in context. This may start at the regional level, considering which are the likely culprits to have left the sign in your location. It may also include knowledge of the behaviour of the animals at that particular time of day or year. For example, if a fresh antler rub on a tree in southern England is found in April, it is most likely to have been done by a roe deer, as this is the time when they really start to become territorial and mark trees. Other deer species that are common in this region, and also commonly thrash trees, have done all their antler rubbing the previous autumn.

Tracking is always a two-part process, whether it's track and sign or trailing that interests you. Firstly, evidence is gathered and then it is used as the basis to reveal the story of what happened. The more one knows about which animals are in the local area, and what they might be doing, then the more accurate and detailed the story can be as to who left the evidence and where they might be now.

It is good to practice zooming in on a piece of evidence, and then zoom out again. It is fascinating how easy it is to lock your focus on a particular track or sign, or even part of a track, and ignore evidence that may only be a short distance away and may be critical in giving you the correct answer. While it is important to pick out detail, it is also important to try to take in the bigger picture.

Beware of becoming 'focus locked'. At first glance, this long, thin track may cause a good deal of head scratching. Pulling back reveals a stick that fits the impression perfectly.

TRACK GROUPS

Described below are the animals most likely to be confused with each other, and specifically what to compare to have the best chance of a positive identification.

PLANTIGRADES

RODENTS

The indicative 'three toes in a row' of this grey squirrel typifies small rodents.

SMALLER RODENTS

Rodents are identified in track terms as showing four toes in the front track, and five in the rear. Some species in this group may show a vestigial fifth toe, which is always toe number one, or the thumb. This toe is so unreliable in terms of its likelihood of showing in the track that we can discount it. However, it will often show in the largest of our rodents, the Eurasian beaver.

The rear tracks of our smaller rodents are very distinctive in that they have toes two, three and four arranged more or less in a straight line in the middle of the track, with toes one and five set out to the sides. The interdigital pads are separate, not massed together as in some mammal species. They can show in the tracks, as can carpal pads on front tracks and the heel on the rear. However, the tiny dots that make up individual interdigital pads are not especially distinct in most substrates – look out especially for two big interdigital pads supporting the three central rear toes and, less frequently, one supporting each of toes one and five. Interdigital pads on the front tend to show as more of a crescent-shaped mass.

I have spent a great deal of time running captive animals across ink, clay and sand traps to find some diagnostic features to separate the tracks of what have previously been regarded, in tracking terms, as unidentifiable species. I have a few observations from this work I would like to share.

Mice and Rats Versus Voles

In good quality substrates tail drag for these species may also be visible.

Mice and rats tend toward having long, slender fingers with quite small toe pads. They also tend to have an asymmetrical arrangement of toes on the front track, with toe five (the little finger) causing the asymmetry by dropping down further. Another way of putting this is that the distance is the same between toe two and toe three as it is between toe three and toe four, but is greater between toe four and toe five.

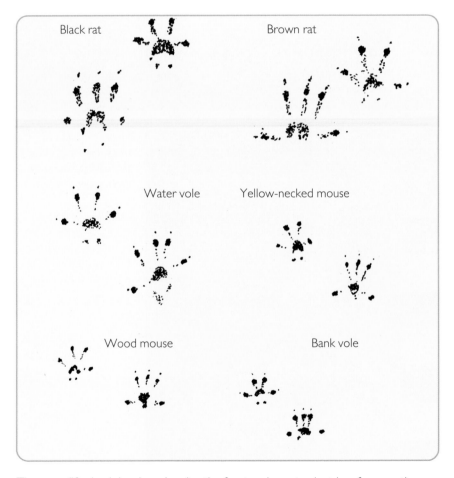

These are life-sized drawings showing the front and rear tracks taken from captive animals that have been run across ink.

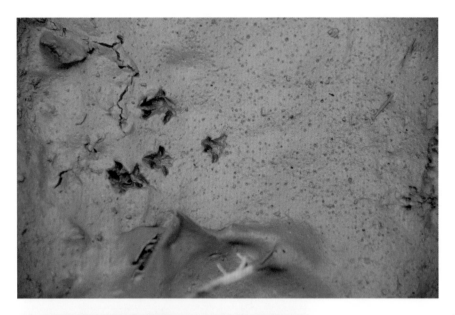

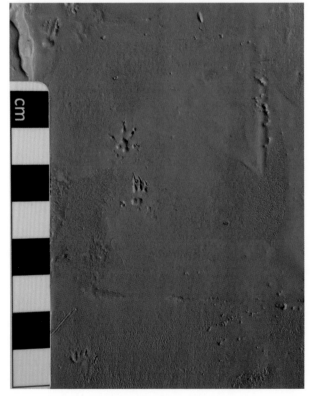

Above: Even in soft mud, the short, stubby toes of the bank vole can be identified.

Left: Front and rear tracks of a bank vole. Note the symmetry on the front track and the relatively short toes.

The rear tracks of mice and rats tend to be symmetrical, in terms of the three central toes being equally spaced apart.

Voles of all sizes have front and rear tracks that are closer in size than rats and mice, whose rear tracks are significantly larger than their fronts.

Voles tend towards having short, stubby fingers and quite large toe pads. The rear tracks of voles normally show the three central toes spaced asymmetrically, with toes three and four closer together than toes two and three. The field vole is an exception to the vole rule as it has toes very similar to mice in terms of length and delicacy of the toe pads, and is of a size that makes it comparable to a yellow-necked mouse. However, the field vole does still tend to show symmetrical front tracks.

When trying to gauge the length of the toes, try to imagine how many toe pad lengths it takes to reach the interdigital pads. With a bank vole, for example, it might be as few as two (because the toe pads are large and the toe length short) and with one of the mice species it could be three or more (with small toe pads and relatively longer toes).

Rats, mice and voles have a tendency to either bound or trot as they move about, although voles seem to prefer trotting, while mice prefer bounding.

Black Rat Versus Brown Rat

Black rats have similar track features to the brown rat and the mice described above, but their fingers are much shorter and stubbier.

Brown Rat Versus Water Vole

The reliable separation of these species would appear to be the holy grail of riparian (river bank) mammal surveying, as water voles are a Species of Conservation Concern with many problems facing them, so knowledge of their presence is very helpful to their conservation.

The water vole's asymmetrical rear feet and symmetrical front feet (opposite to the symmetry in both the brown and the much rarer black rat) works to help separate these species. Also, the toes tend to spread wider in water vole tracks, giving them a star-shaped appearance. Toe one on the rear foot of a water vole often 'drops out', being positioned further back like the thumb on a human hand. The three central toes on the

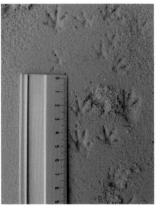

Above left: Brown rat tracks showing symmetry in the rear track (top left) and asymmetry in the front track.

Above right: Note the 'star'-shaped and symmetrical four-toed front tracks of this water vole. It is not so obvious here, but the rear track, closest to the ruler, shows some slight asymmetry with toes three and four closer together. (MB)

Three toes in a row from the rear foot of a brown rat.

water vole track may also not be in such an obvious line as with a brown rat, as they splay further and form an arc.

Look also for other evidence of feeding, droppings and burrows. If you find clear brown rat tracks and sign, especially in large quantities, it is very unlikely that water voles will also be present, as they really don't like rats as neighbours. Keep in mind that if tracking near a body of water that is popular with picnickers or where people feed water birds, then rats are likely to be attracted to these spots.

Yellow-Necked Mouse Versus Field Vole

The yellow-necked mouse is generally a bigger animal than the wood mouse, by at least 20 per cent, although this may mean little when young animals are about in the summer.

The yellow-necked mouse does have a consistent tendency to show toe one and toe five on the rear track set far behind the interdigital pads.

The tracks of these two species can look superficially similar but still show the mouse/vole distinctions mentioned above.

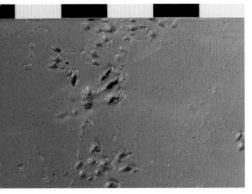 

Above left: Note the toes set further back on this yellow-necked mouse compared with the smaller wood mouse. The long, slender toes, especially on the rear track, are also visible. Look for the asymmetry on the lower track.

Above right: Wood mouse tracks.

The right front and rear of a field vole (life-sized).

However, the track descriptions represent 'tendencies' and it is possible for a vole to leave symmetrical rear tracks and vice versa with rats and mice. It is also possible that a wood mouse will place toe one and toe five behind the inter-digital pad in the rear track.

Harvest Mouse

I have included pictures of harvest mouse tracks for content, but in truth I have never found them in the wild and it is unlikely that they are common in the landscape.

House Mouse

The house mouse is actually very rare, and should you experience the delights of having mice in your home, they are most likely to be wood mice.

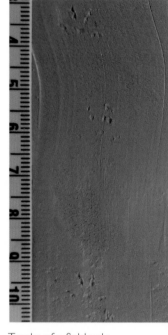

Tracks of a field vole

Life-sized right tracks of a harvest mouse.

Life-sized right tracks of a house mouse.

Bounding trail of a black rat. See the section on gaits and track patterns.

Trotting trail of a water vole. See the section on gaits and track patterns.

House mouse tracks are very much like a smaller version of wood mouse tracks in their toe arrangement.

Species	Rear L x W (cm) +/−	Front L x W (cm) +/−
Black rat (*Rattus rattus*)	1.6 x 1.6	1.1 x 1.6
Brown rat (*Rattus norvegicus*)	1.6 x 2.2	1.4 x 1.7
Water vole (*Arvicola amphibious*)	1.4 x 1.2	1.0 x 1.5
Yellow-necked mouse (*Apodemus flavicollis*)	0.9 x 1.0	0.7 x 1.0
Wood mouse (*Apodemus sylvaticus*)	1.0 x 1.0	1.0 x 0.9
Bank vole (*Myodes glareolus*)	0.7 x 0.9	0.7 x 0.9
Field vole (*Microtus agrestis*)	1.0 x 1.0	0.8 x 1.0
House mouse (*Mus musculus*)	0.6 x 0.7	0.6 x 0.6
Harvest mouse (*Micromys minutus*)	0.5 x 0.6	0.5 x 0.5

NB: There are a couple of island subspecies of the common vole: Guernsey vole (*Microtus arvalis sarnius*); and Orkney vole (*Microtus arvalis orcadensis*). We also have the Skomer vole (*Myodes glareolus skomerensis*). I do not currently have data on the common vole subspecies, but the Skomer vole is a subspecies of the bank vole and I would imagine its tracks are very similar, if not identical to the mainland form.

Dormice

We have two (unrelated) species of dormice in the UK: our native hazel dormouse and the introduced edible dormouse. The former is a regular-sized 'mouse', while the latter is more rat- or even squirrel-sized.

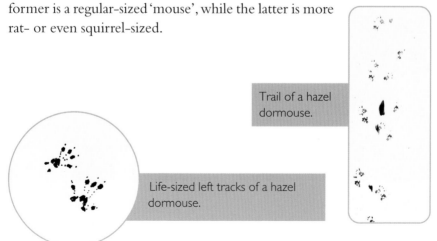

Trail of a hazel dormouse.

Life-sized left tracks of a hazel dormouse.

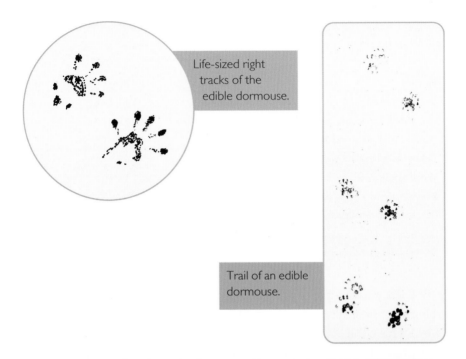

Life-sized right tracks of the edible dormouse.

Trail of an edible dormouse.

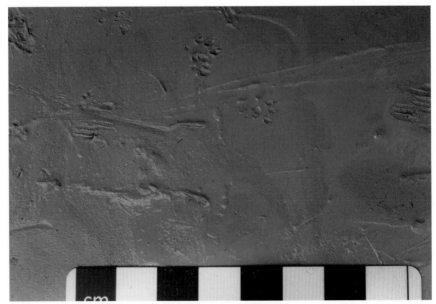

Tracks of the hazel dormouse.

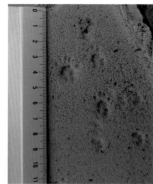

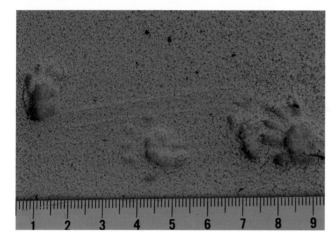

Above left: Tracks of the hazel dormouse.

Above right: Tracks of an edible dormouse. (MB)

Left: Tracks of an edible dormouse. (MB)

Distinctively, the tracks of both these species show toes ahead of the palm pads, like a miniature badger track. The hazel dormouse tends to orientate its feet towards the outside of the trail – this always makes me think of how a chameleon would walk. It is extremely rare to find the tracks of a hazel dormouse on the ground, but not impossible. Increasingly, ink traps are being used to survey for these animals and I include a trail in ink for comparison (see page 47).

The edible dormouse exhibits these same characteristics but is much larger and doesn't point its feet out to the same degree, although enough that these characteristics should make it easier to separate from other large rodents, especially squirrels.

Both species of dormice tend to walk or bound.

Species	Rear L x W (cm) +/–	Front L x W (cm) +/–
Edible dormouse (*Glis glis*)	1.5 x 1.7	1.1 x 1.3
Hazel dormouse (*Muscardinus avellanarius*)	0.8 x 0.9	0.6 x 0.5

Squirrels

There are two species of squirrel in the UK, our native red squirrel and the introduced American eastern grey squirrel. Their tracks are very difficult, if not impossible, to tell apart. The tracks of the grey squirrel are a little larger and more robust, although this difference can be very subjective.

Red squirrels tend to register the rear interdigital pad less strongly than the grey, but this is very variable depending on substrate.

They both show the typical four toes on the front foot and five on the rear and are the largest rodents exhibiting this characteristic that you are likely to come across. They are nearly twice as large as rat tracks. The interdigital pads are separated into three separate pads on the front and four on the rear, but generally they show as a solid mass in the track. In

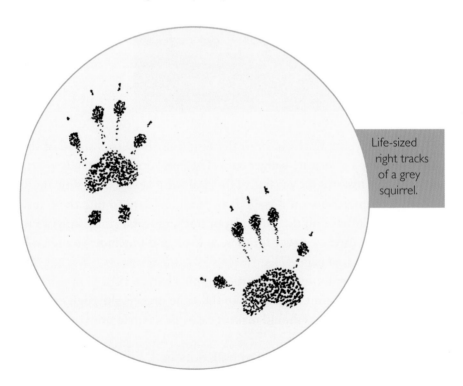

Life-sized right tracks of a grey squirrel.

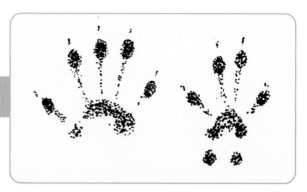

Life-sized right tracks of a red squirrel.

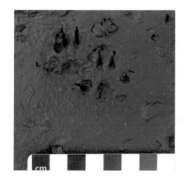

Above left: Grey squirrel left tracks with rear above, front below.

Above right: Grey squirrel tracks in mud showing the typical arrangement of the feet.

good substrate, two separate carpal pads show distinctly as little circles. The interdigital mass on the rear track slopes gently towards toe one, and more steeply towards toe five, which makes it possible to distinguish left and right tracks. In both front and rear tracks, toe four is the leading toe, which again helps determine which side of the body they are from. An impression from the vestigial toe one may also be visible on the front track in good substrate. See the section on Foot Morphology above.

The typical gait of a squirrel is to bound and hop, and most typically show the two front tracks side by side with the two hinds set outside of these tracks. This parallel placement of the front feet distinguishes them from lagomorphs and can be seen in the muddy photo above.

The grey squirrel is by far the most common of the two squirrel species across the UK.

Species	Rear L x W (cm) +/ −	Front L x W (cm) +/ −
Red squirrel (*Sciuris vulgaris*)	2.8 x 2.5	2.3 x 2.4
Grey squirrel (*Sciuris carolinensis*)	2.8 x 2.5	2.3 x 2.4

LARGE RODENTS

Eurasian Beaver

Eurasian beaver tracks are unmistakable in the UK as there is nothing else exhibiting their size and shape. In mainland Europe, there is potential confusion between the beaver and the introduced coypu, which in the UK was eradicated as an invasive species in the 1980s. The thumb of the beaver may register weakly in the front tracks, while in the rear tracks toe three and toe four are often all that is visible. Webbing may sometimes show. Beavers also have a tendency to direct register as they walk, with the rear track then obliterating all or most of the front track.

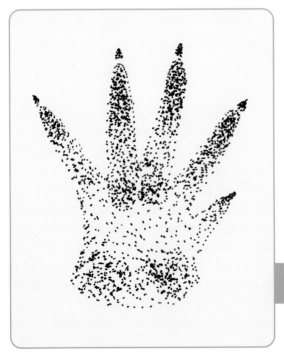

Life-sized front left track of a beaver.

52

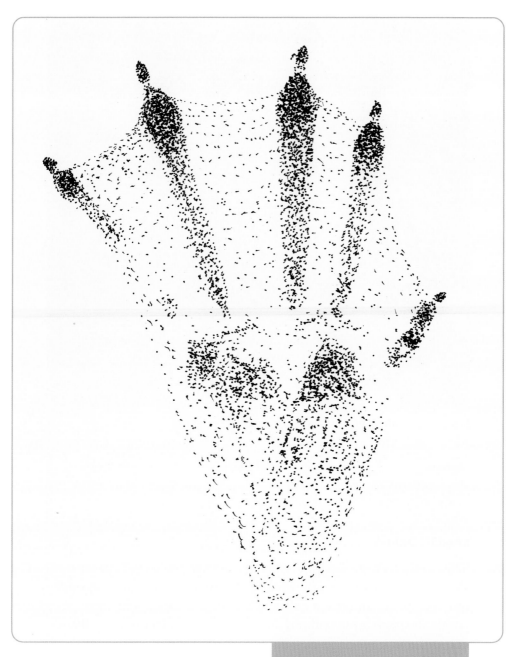

Life-sized rear left track of a beaver.

Beaver track with rear foot partially obscuring the front. (RN)

Species	Rear L x W (cm) +/ –	Front L x W (cm) +/ –
Eurasian beaver (*Castor fiber*)	15 x 10.5	6.5 x 5.5

LAGOMORPHS

This family of creatures is represented by our rabbits and two hare species, all of which have five toes showing on the front feet but only four on the rear. Toe one on the front is set far back in the foot, and often doesn't register in the track. Even without this toe to help in identification, the rest of the toes arch round to the outside of the track in an inverted 'J' shape. The leading toe on the front track is toe three, which also helps determine left and right in a trail.

The rear tracks are more symmetrical and can be confused with those of the red fox in certain substrates. This is compounded by what looks like the fox's palm pad chevron which frequently shows in hare tracks. However, closer inspection often reveals a certain asymmetry that makes the track look slightly skewed, and when this is the case, toe three is the leading toe.

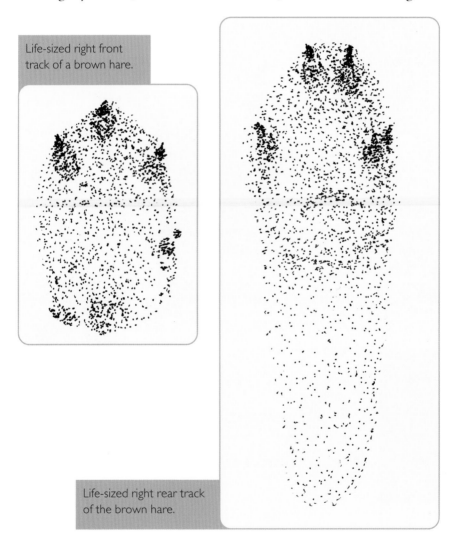

Life-sized right front track of a brown hare.

Life-sized right rear track of the brown hare.

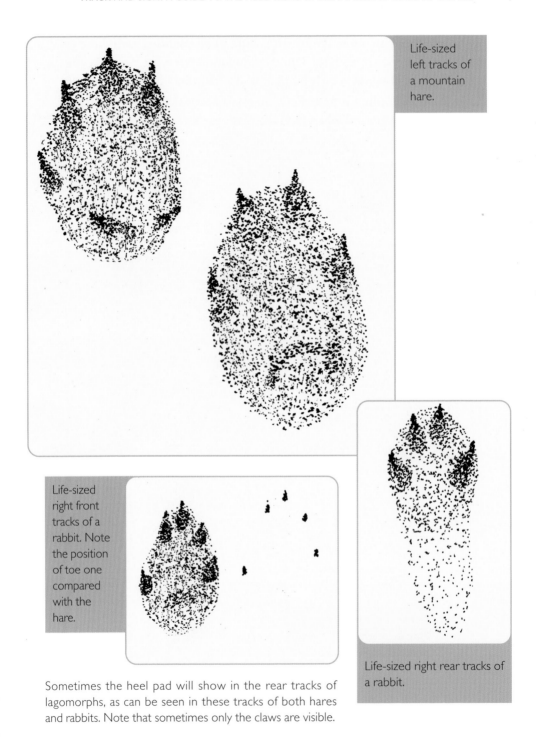

Life-sized left tracks of a mountain hare.

Life-sized right front tracks of a rabbit. Note the position of toe one compared with the hare.

Life-sized right rear tracks of a rabbit.

Sometimes the heel pad will show in the rear tracks of lagomorphs, as can be seen in these tracks of both hares and rabbits. Note that sometimes only the claws are visible.

Above left: The hairy foot of a brown hare.

Above right: Clothes moths revealed the detail of the toes and claws of this mountain hare foot.

Right: Front right track of a brown hare.

All lagomorph species in the UK have no toe or interdigital pads to show, instead having feet covered in stiff hairs. Often there is only the faintest impression of the toe bones in the track, or simply the compression shape of the foot. Sometimes in hard substrates only the claws will show. This variety of presentations is why lagomorph tracks may be confused with a variety of other animals.

Rear tracks of all species may show the entire heel pad, especially if the animal stops and sits.

NB: Toe number one is frequently faint in the front tracks, and always absent in the rear tracks of all species.

Above left: Rear track of a brown hare showing the heel.

Above right: A mountain hare track. (DP)

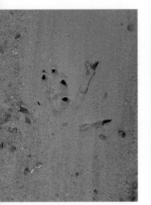  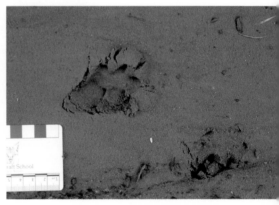

Above left: Front right track of a rabbit on top of a pheasant track.

Above centre: Rabbit rear tracks with just claws showing.

Above right: The sharp turn of this rabbit shows in the energy transferred to the substrate.

Left: A nice set of rabbit tracks showing the furry feet.

Hare Versus European Rabbit

In addition to the size difference, which is helpful, it can be fairly easy to distinguish rabbits from hares in their tracks. When toe one is present, its position relative to toe five is diagnostic in separating hares and rabbits. This is something that was first explained to me by José Galán, a very talented Spanish tracker and CyberTracker evaluator. In rabbit tracks, toe one and toe five are almost in line with each other, whereas in hares, toe one is set much further back in the track.

Brown Hare Versus Mountain Hare

These two species can be difficult to separate from their tracks, and location may be helpful. In England, there are very few places where both species occur. Generally speaking though, the tracks of the mountain hare are slightly shorter but broader than those of the brown hare, and in snow they are capable of spreading out to a surprising degree.

Hare Versus Red Fox

Look for the triangular shape to toes two and five on a fox track and for the more asymmetrical hare track.

Gait: Lagomorphs tend to hop or bound, and their trails can, at first sight, be confusing. Their rear feet move ahead of the fronts, which are placed one in front of the other. A set of four tracks can give the impression that the animal was travelling in entirely the opposite direction to the one it was actually moving in. When moving slowly, this reaching past the fronts with the rear legs may not occur. See Gaits and Track Patterns.

The typical gait of a running brown hare. Both rear tracks in the left of the photo.

Species	Rear L x W (cm) +/ −	Front L x W (cm) +/ −
European rabbit (*Oryctolagus cuniculus*)	3.5 x 2.5	3.5 x 2.3
Brown hare (*Lepus europaeus*)	6.0 x 4.0	6.0 x 3.5
Mountain hare (*Lepus timidus*)	6.0 x 4.4	5.5 x 4.0

INSECTIVORES

The feet of insectivores have five toes on the front feet and five on the rear, all of which are capable of showing in the tracks. As is often the case with all of our five-toed mammals, the thumb or toe one frequently doesn't show in the track, and so cannot be relied upon for identification. Some animals in this group are exceptionally small and their tracks can be quite difficult to find.

Shrews

We have five species of shrew in the UK, the water shrew (*Neomys fodiens*) being the largest and the pygmy shrew (*Sorex minutus*) the smallest in the family. The two *Sorex* species, the common shrew (*S. Araneus*) and pygmy shrew are the most commonly encountered. The two *Crocidura* shrews are the greater white-toothed shrew (*C. russula*), which is only found in Ireland, and the lesser white-toothed shrew (*C. suaveolens*), which is found only on the Isles of Scilly.

The most commonly encountered shrew tracks will be of the common shrew and perhaps the pygmy shrew, although for me personally it means getting down on my hands and knees to even see them – they are extremely small.

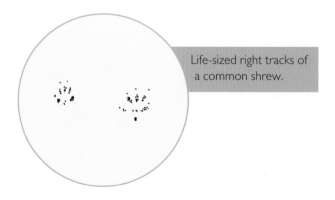

Life-sized right tracks of a common shrew.

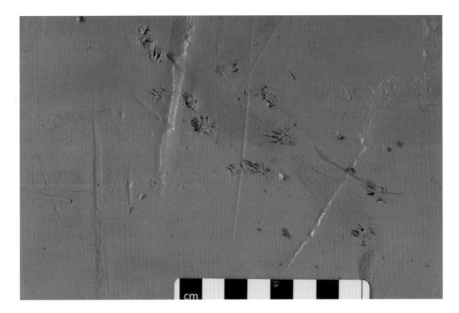

Shrew tracks.

Shrews Versus Small Rodents

Compared to small mice species, the toes in shrew tracks can be so fine as to look like coarse hair with relatively small, almost unnoticeable, toe pads. The arrangement of toes is similar to rodent rear feet in both front and back tracks, but the front tracks appear narrower than the rear. If toe one isn't showing in the track, look for asymmetry in the four toes that have registered to help in identification. The front feet of mice, with their four toes, look symmetrical (aside from the dropped toe five described above). Tracks of the pygmy shrew are, as you would expect, smaller than those of the common shrew. Fine claws may also show, possibly because of how soft the substrate needs to be to register them.

Gait: Shrews tend to trot.

HEDGEHOGS

These curious creatures are sadly getting rarer in the UK, having declined significantly in numbers in recent years. On their front tracks, toe one is frequently absent, and they can then look superficially like rat or squirrel tracks.

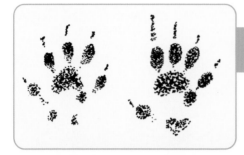

Life-sized right tracks of a hedgehog.

Below: Hedgehog tracks. Note the long claw on the rear foot.

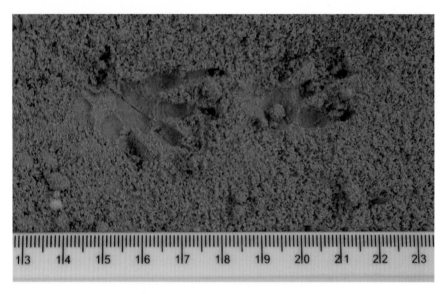

Far left: Front right foot of a hedgehog.

Left: Rear foot of a hedgehog.

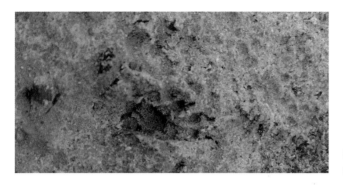

Partial rear track of a hedgehog.

Hedgehogs Versus Rats

Look for short fingers with quite long, sometimes almost oval toe pads, especially in comparison to the rodents. The five toes on the front track are arranged in an arc and never present as the classic three leading toes in a row of rodent rear tracks. If toe one is absent the track can look very asymmetric and skewed to the side.

On the rear tracks, if toe one shows at all, it is set back. What is often distinctive, though, is the long nail on toe two which extends further than any of the other nails. Presumably this is a grooming claw, and is long to enable reaching between the spines.

Gait: Hedgehogs tend to walk, with rear tracks often directly registering on the fronts.

Wide walking trail of a hedgehog. See the section on gaits and track patterns.

EUROPEAN MOLE

The presence of European moles can be most readily noticed by the conspicuous mounds of earth they leave behind. They do, very occasionally, move around above ground, and I have encountered them when either the ground is very dry and hard to dig through, or when their tunnels become flooded. In both instances they will migrate to more favourable burrowing terrain. I have also encountered them above ground when sick or injured.

Their unusual tracks are most likely to be confused with those of a toad. Mole front tracks are very distinctive due to their highly adapted digging function. Five toes may register, but more classically it is three together with perhaps a fainter fourth toe visible in an arcing line of dots pointing out from the centre of the trail.

Rear tracks may look similar to those of small rodents, with three central toes and toe one and toe five out to the sides. Close inspection should reveal an arc in these central toes rather than a row of toes in line.

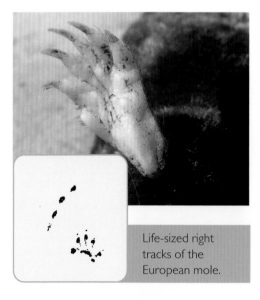

Life-sized right tracks of the European mole.

Mole feet showing the contrast between the large spade-like front feet and the smaller rear feet. (RA)

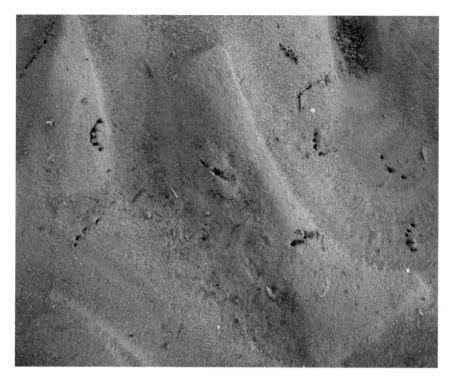

These are the tracks of a North American mole species but are very similar to our European mole. (BM)

Moles Versus Toads

The confusion between these two species is usually because of the arrangement of toes on the toad's rear foot, with the mole's front feet leaving a similar line of dots. However, the hind tracks of a mole point in the direction of travel but a toad's front tracks point at 90 degrees from the direction of travel, towards the centre of the trail.

Gait: Moles tend to walk.

Species	Rear L x W (cm) +/ −	Front L x W (cm) +/ −
Common shrew (*Sorex araneus*)	0.5 x 0.7	0.4 x 0.5
European mole (*Talpa europaea*)	0.7 x 0.9	1.4 x 1.0
Eurasian hedgehog (*Erinaceus europaeus*)	1.8 x 2.0	2.5 x 2.2

MUSTELIDS

The mustelids represent the largest group of carnivores in our region and include (in ascending order of size) the weasel, stoat, polecat/ferret, American mink, pine marten, otter and badger. With the exception of the badger, the foot structure of these animals is very similar, with five toes on both the front and the rear, arranged in an arc around a central interdigital pad.

Once again, toe one may not show, and in several species it is set further back on the rear foot than the front. If toe one isn't showing, look for asymmetry in the track which often points to the space where toe one should be. This can also be seen in the asymmetry of the interdigital pad which indicates where toe one is located. The interdigital pads comprise three similar-sized pads fused together, with a fourth pad set further back and associated with toe one. The interdigital pads may show as a joined-up, continuous pad or each separately, dependent on substrate.

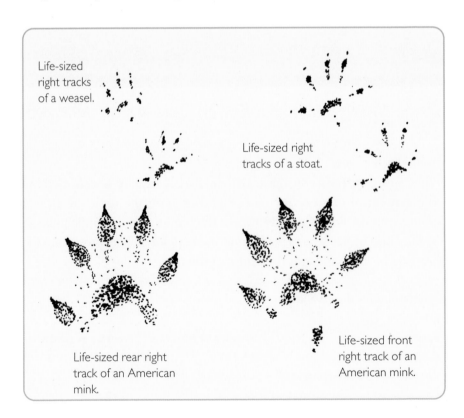

Life-sized right tracks of a weasel.

Life-sized right tracks of a stoat.

Life-sized rear right track of an American mink.

Life-sized front right track of an American mink.

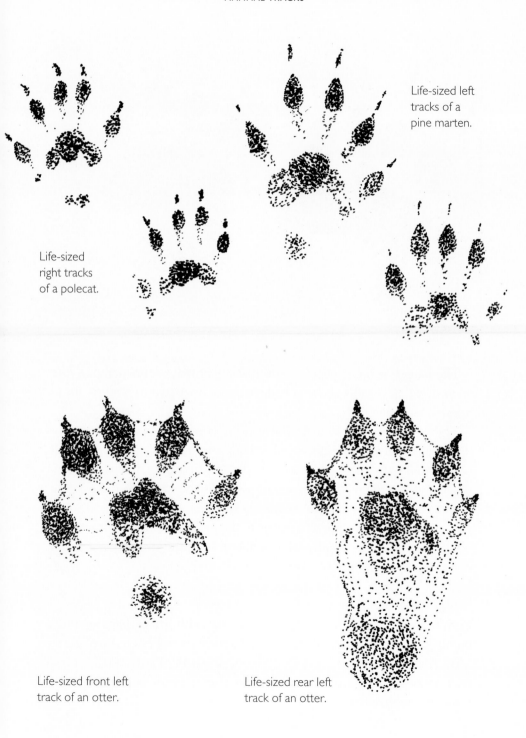

MAMMAL TRACKS

Life-sized left
tracks of a
pine marten.

Life-sized
right tracks
of a polecat.

Life-sized front left
track of an otter.

Life-sized rear left
track of an otter.

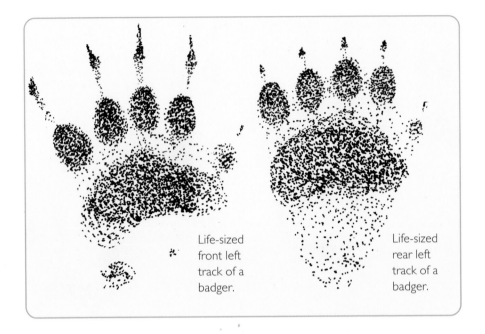

Life-sized front left track of a badger.

Life-sized rear left track of a badger.

The badger is the exception to the arrangement outlined above. The main toes that reliably show in badger tracks (toes two to five) sit ahead of the interdigital pad.

There is size-based sexual dimorphism in mustelids, with the males significantly larger than the females. Therefore, there can be a potential overlap in the size of tracks between males and females of different species.

The claws in mustelids often register some distance away from the end of the toe pad in all but the softest of substrates. The exception to this is the otter where the claws often appear 'attached' to the toes in a similar way to dogs.

NB: Toe one is frequently faint or absent in both front and rear tracks of all mustelid species.

Weasel and Stoat

Both of these species leave very similar tracks, with size perhaps the most useful guide in separating them. A small female weasel can leave tracks as small as some of our larger mice species, but equally I have run a captive male weasel over ink that has left tracks that are very similar in size to those of a captive female stoat.

 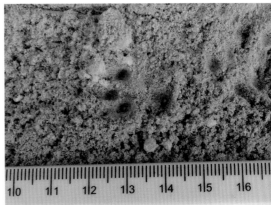

Above left: Weasel tracks are very hard to find.

Above right: Even with an incomplete track, the spacing of the toes and asymmetry points to a mustelid track.

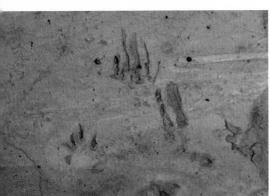

Above left: Weasel track showing all five toes.

Above right: Nice set of stoat tracks, moving in a lope that's common to mustelids.

Left: Stoat tracks showing where it has slipped in the mud.

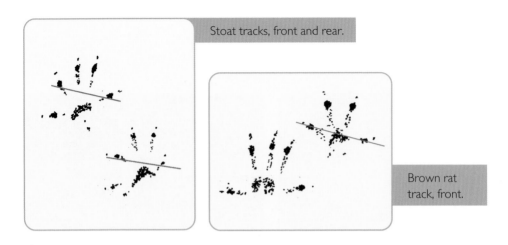

Stoat tracks, front and rear.

Brown rat track, front.

Weasel and Stoat Versus Rodents

The main confusion between these small mustelids and rodents comes about when toe one doesn't show, making a Stoat or weasel track look like the four-toed front track of a rodent. A nice trick to try is to imagine a straight line running under the two outermost toes that you can see. In rodents, this line will cut through or intersect the interdigital pad, and in a small mustelid it will pass above it. This line rule can also be very helpful in identifying the tracks of larger mustelids.

POLECAT AND AMERICAN MINK

Polecats are, at the time of writing, on the increase after a decline in the persecution they have been subjected to for decades. They are now spreading out rapidly from their stronghold in the west of the country. Their tracks are indistinguishable from feral/escaped ferrets and are most likely to be confused with American mink, the other similar-sized mustelid, especially when considering the sexual dimorphism of this group. Both species are very similar and exhibit the classic mustelid features described above.

American Mink Versus Polecat

American mink tracks are very similar to those of polecats, but their front tracks are proportionately wider, giving them a star-shaped appearance. The impression is one of all the toes pointing in different directions. The claws are quite fine when present in the track, and in soft substrates partial webbing of the feet may be visible, this being absent in other mustelids of a similar size.

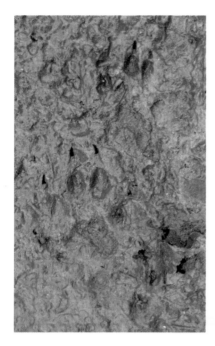

Above: A nice set of polecat tracks showing good detail due to the substrate.

Above left: Polecat tracks. Note how the interdigital pad supporting toe one is separate.

Above right: Polecat tracks in slightly harder substrate.

Above left: American mink tracks. Note the spread in the front track and the more compact rear track to the right.

Above right: Classic mustelid lope but with the American mink's spreading front tracks still obvious. See the section on gaits and track patterns.

In polecat tracks, the distances between the toes are smaller, making the track appear particularly compact. This is the most reliable distinguishing feature in my experience. Polecats also have more obvious claws which may curve and show in the tracks reliably. The interdigital pad extends down further towards toe one than in mink, but this can be difficult to see in the track.

PINE MARTEN

Pine marten tracks are much bigger and more robust than those of the American mink or polecat, but depending on the time of year, their toe pads may appear small in relation to the overall size of the track. This is due to their hairy feet, which are more prominent in winter. Pine martens have thin, sharp claws that are adapted for climbing and these frequently show in their tracks.

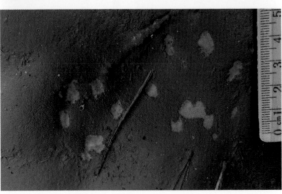

Left: Front track of a pine marten. (BO)

Below left: Set of tracks of a pine marten. Look for toe one to get right or left, and size for rear and front. (RN)

Below right: Perfect pine marten trail. (RN)

Although this is not illustrated in my drawing, in good substrates, a second smaller carpal pad may be visible on the front track, close to the inside of the trail. However, as with carpal pads in general, this very often doesn't show. Pine marten toes are long, leaving a large negative space between the carpal pad and toe pads.

Pine Marten Versus Polecat

Although it is difficult to tell, in some instances, due to size differences with adults and juveniles, adult pine marten tracks are bigger than those of the polecat. Other distinctions are as mentioned above and are related to their claws, negative space indicating longer fingers and the presence or absence of hair.

OTTER

The otter has all the features of a giant mustelid and also frequently shows webbing between the toes. However, this is not necessarily a given and should not be relied on too much in identification. Otter front tracks are noticeably wider and rounder than their rear tracks, and they show more space between the toes.

Frequently, although it is classically mustelid-shaped, the interdigital pad often only shows the highest, broadest segment that has a surface area equivalent to one and a half toe pads. Even when the other elements of the interdigital pad registers, this is still the deepest part of the track. Carpal pads show regularly, but this is possibly due to the softer substrates these tracks are most often found in.

Above left: Otter – front foot on the left, rear on the right

Above right: Left front and rear tracks of an otter in perfect relief. (MB)

73

The narrow rear tracks often show the heel pad. Toes are robust with thick, blunt claws that frequently show, and are in close proximity to the toe pads, making them look dog-like.

Otter Versus Dog

The toe and claw combination make otter toes look very like those of dogs, leading to potential confusion when toe one is absent in the track. Look closely at the outer toes and check for any hint of the triangular shape often found with canids. Also, the depth and size of the interdigital pad is useful. In dogs, it is large in relation to the overall size of the track and triangular in shape and it doesn't normally register as deeply as in an otter.

Otter Versus Cat

Otter claws may not register in the track, thus giving rise to potential confusion with cats. Also, cats will regularly register their claws, but these are thin and needle-like and do not normally present in the track as attached to the toe in the same way that they do in otter tracks. Cat toes are small in relation to the overall compression of the track and the inter-digital pad is blocky and symmetrical, as described in the following pages.

Gait: The mustelids described so far tend to trot or use the 2 x 2 or 3 x 4 rotary lope.

Below left: Note the blunt claws in these otter tracks.

Below right: These tracks are not so obvious, but the features identifying this as an otter are there if studied closely.

Above left: A perfect pair of badger tracks with toe one showing.

Above right: Note how far ahead of the toe pads the claws register.

Left: This badger track shows the difference between claw length on the front and rear feet.

BADGER

Badger tracks are unique among the mustelid tracks. On both rear and front feet, toes two to five are arranged in a gentle curve ahead of the large, blocky interdigital pad. Toe five often shows as the largest toe, and if toe one registers, it is set behind and slightly to the side of the other toes. In both sexes, the rear tracks are small and narrow compared to the fronts and have noticeably shorter claws compared to the fronts, on which the claws are exceptionally long and broader. Carpal pads in the front track and heel pads in the rear will register in very soft substrate, as will the full length of the claws. The claws are curved and, in front tracks, are very long and can therefore register as dots well ahead of the toe pads. In hard substrates it may only be the tips of the claws that register, with no pads at all.

The large, blocky interdigital pad narrows slightly to the inside of the trail, and especially so on the front track. This is a good feature in determining left and right tracks.

Above left: Without claws showing, badger tracks can be mistaken for cat tracks. Note the more rectangular palm pad and the concave lower edge.

Above right: A badger in a direct-registered walking gait.

Badger Versus Cats And Dogs

Occasionally, the toes on a badger track appear to arch to the point where those of a young badger can look superficially like cat tracks. This is especially true if the badger's claws do not register or go unnoticed. Carefully check the shape of the interdigital pad which, as described above, is much more rectangular in a badger in comparison to the squarer and symmetrical pad of a cat. Cats should show toes two and five below the leading edge of the interdigital pad. Badgers may, on occasion, look like 'cat-footed' dogs (see below) – look for the absence of triangular outer toes that indicate a badger.

Front left foot of a badger showing the long digging claws and the carpal pad.

Gait: Badgers tend to walk or trot but can gallop when they feel the need.

Species	Rear L x W (cm) +/ −	Front L x W (cm) +/ −
Weasel (*Mustela nivalis*)	0.9 x 1.4	0.8 x 1.0
Stoat (*Mustela erminea*)	1.4 x 2.0	1.2 x 1.8
American mink (*Neovison vison*)	3.0 x 3.5	2.5 x 3.4
Polecat/ferret (*Mustela putorius/furo*)	3.0 x 2.8	3.0 x 3.0
Pine marten (*Martes martes*)	3.2 x 3.2	4.0 x 3.8
Otter (*Lutra lutra*)	4.0 x 4.5	4.2 x 5.2
Badger (*Meles meles*)	3.8 x 4.5	4.3 x 5.0

DIGITIGRADES

FELIDS

Cats generally show the same features across each of the various species. Their front tracks are rounder and wider than the rear and are often wider than they are long. The front track is much more asymmetrical than the rear and may look as though it is skewed from the obvious line of travel. Toe three is the longest if there is a difference, and some tracks can show toes three, four and five in a gentle arcing line with toe two off to the side.

The toes of cats are tiny in relation to the overall track compression, and also in relation to the interdigital pad. All of the toe pads would almost fit inside the area of the large interdigital pad. Rear tracks are more symmetrical and appear longer than they are wide.

The front and rear interdigital pads have three lobes on the trailing edge, and two on the leading edge, and this shows regularly in the track. The rear interdigital pad is narrower on its leading edge than in the front track. When the three lobes on the trailing edge do not show, an apparent curve across the proximal edge of the interdigital pad is often evident. When they are evident, the lobes are more or less in line.

Claws (which are evolved for holding prey and climbing) will frequently show in the track as fine needle points. Toe one is found high up the leg on the front and may show in soft ground and/or when the animal is moving fast. There are normally only four toes on the rear, but some domestic cats have a dew claw here as well. Carpal pads and heels may also show in the tracks.

DOMESTIC CAT

Domestic cats show all the classic features as describe above but occasionally have rear feet larger than the fronts. They can also be polydactyly, and so may show an extra toe in the track. They are generally smaller than the other felids likely to be encountered but this not reliable due to hybridisation (as happens with wildcats), and selective breeding.

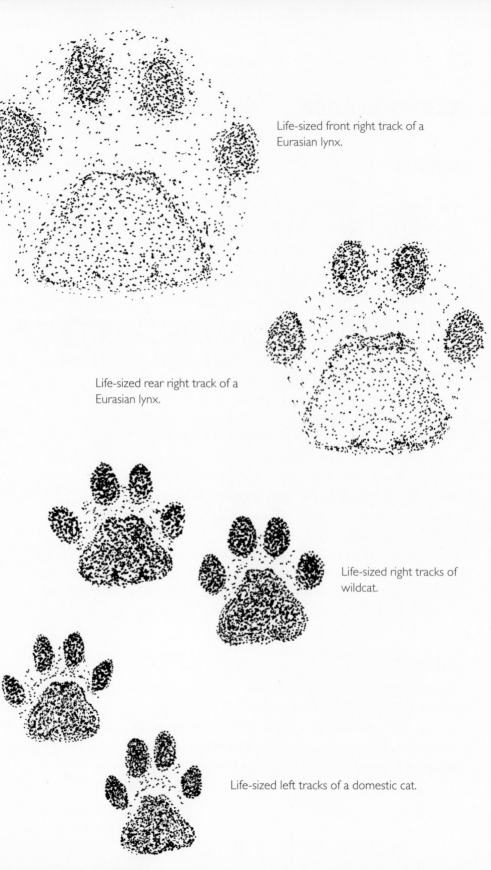

Life-sized front right track of a Eurasian lynx.

Life-sized rear right track of a Eurasian lynx.

Life-sized right tracks of wildcat.

Life-sized left tracks of a domestic cat.

Above left: There are several cat tracks in this image showing the asymmetry and a hint of the lobes on the palm pad.

Above right: This is an old track and so is slightly blown out, but the wide round shape and the hint of three lobes on the palm pad are still indicative of a front cat track travelling left to right.

Above left: Compact and more symmetrical, this is of the same cat, but as well as shape it shows a difference in size between rear and front tracks.

Above right: Perfect pair of domestic cat right tracks, front track to the top of the photo. (DW.)

WILDCAT

Unfortunately, this predator is, at time of writing, under serious threat of extinction in the UK. Some authorities would suggest it is, in fact, already biologically extinct with too few true wildcats to form a viable population. This is primarily due to centuries of over-hunting to protect game and farm stock, and through hybridisation with domestic cats.

Left: Front left track of a wildcat.

Below left: A wildcat's regular travel route. (IM)

Below right: Wildcat foot. (IM)

Wildcat tracks look like a bigger, more robust domestic cat, but of course this becomes very subjective. A pure-bred wildcat tom track might be at least 20 per cent bigger than that of a domestic cat, but there is clearly a large overlap, especially when considering hybrids which vary considerably as to the proportion of wildcat and domestic cat genes they carry. There are also some huge domestic cat breeds, and as the habitat of wildcats overlaps with that of domestic cats then other track and sign clues may be needed to verify the identification.

There are moves to reintroduce wildcats using captive-bred and/ or wild European wildcats that are genetically almost identical to our Scottish subspecies. It is therefore possible that they may once again become common.

Studies with GPS-collared wildcats would suggest that where the tracks are found might be the most reliable way of identifying them. It seems that the wilder the cat, the more it keeps to the shadows, hugging hedge lines and scrub, and avoiding open ground.

Cats Versus Pine Marten and Polecat

Confusion between cats and similar-sized mustelids is possible, but generally the tips of the toes of cats are rounder than those of polecats and pine martens, both of which have toe pads that are more egg-shaped, being thinner at the tip. It is usually the asymmetry of the front track of a cat that throws the identification into doubt. With this in mind, check the relative positions of the other toes as described above. The negative space is larger in the pine marten, so take note of the distance between the back of the toe pads and the front of the interdigital pad. If the interdigital pad shows in the cat, it will be large and blocky, and more or less symmetrical.

EUROPEAN LYNX

The European lynx exhibits a fairly typical cat foot structure, just on a much larger scale, such that it is most likely to be confused with a dog or perhaps a large male (dog) otter. Check carefully the size of the toes relative to the interdigital pad to distinguish between these species. There are no other large cats in Northern Europe to confuse it with.

Gait: Cats tend to walk.

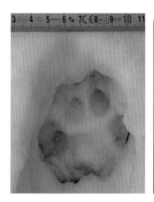
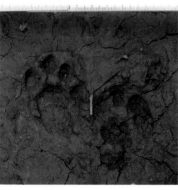

Far left: Lynx rear track on top of the front track. (JK)

Left: Although slightly obscured in the substrate, the features of a large cat are still evident. (JK)

Species	Rear L x W (cm) +/ −	Front L x W (cm) +/ −
Domestic cat (*Felis catus*)	3.2 x 2.7	3.0 x 3.2
Wildcat (*Felis silvestris*)	3.5 x 3.3	3.4 x 3.8
European lynx (*Lynx lynx*)	5.6 x 6.0	6.8 x 7.4

CANIDS

Canid tracks are generally symmetrical but often show toe three as the longest, just like in a human hand. Occasionally, toe two can be higher in the track than toe five, but other than this the tracks tend to show good symmetry. Toes two and five show as triangles with the apexes pointing into the centre of the track, and they are frequently smaller than toes three and four. The toe pads are very robust, and large in relation to the total track size, with perhaps one and a half or two toes fitting into the area of interdigital pad.

Toe one is high up the leg on the front leg and may show in soft ground and/or when the animal is moving fast. There are normally only four toes on the rear track, but some domestic breeds have a dew claw (toe one) here also. The carpal pad on the front track may also show when the animal is travelling at speed or on soft ground.

Rear tracks are long and narrow compared with the rounder and wider fronts, although there is considerable variation with domestic dogs (see below). The interdigital pad is large and triangular with two lobes at each of the lower corners, although these only tend to show as deeper impressions. Canid claws are thick and blunt in dogs and often appear connected to the toe pad in both dogs and, in fact, wolves. This reflects the nature of the canid hunting strategy of running down their prey, with the nails acting mostly as running spikes for improved traction. Some dogs that do not visit either the manicurist or abrasive hard surfaces may have sharper-looking claws.

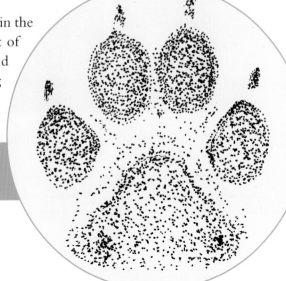

Some features are different in the red fox due to large amount of fur on their feet and the red fox's more cat-like, stalking hunting strategy.

Life-sized domestic dog front left track – the cat foot of a Labrador.

82

DOGS

Domestic dogs have been selectively bred for thousands of years and show considerable variation in the shape of the foot and therefore their tracks. Broadly speaking, the descriptions above apply but with the potential for the following deviations.

Hare Foot

This foot type belongs to the variously named gaze hounds, long dogs and running dogs. In other words, those that rely on keen eyesight and a quick turn of speed, which includes the lurchers, greyhounds and whippets. The two leading toes, toes three and four, are elongated, presumably for speed, which causes toes two and five to tuck in behind, in some cases directly behind. The track takes on a much narrower and elongated appearance.

Cat Foot

The cat foot type is characteristic of working dogs such as Airedales, Labradors and akitas, dogs bred for endurance. They are almost opposite to the hare foot configuration in that the toes are short and compact, and arranged in a cat-like pattern. It is thought that less energy is involved in repeatedly lifting feet of this shape over long periods of time.

Oval Foot

These seem to be the general-purpose feet of choice for dogs that are not extremely specialised in either sprinting or long-distance running. It could be that this foot type is closest to the design of the wild canids, as wolves also have these features. The toe pads are arranged in a more widely spaced arch around the interdigital pad giving the whole track compression an oval appearance. Many dogs have an oval front foot with a rear foot tending to be hare-footed.

Hairy Foot

Some breeds like huskies have extremely hairy feet resulting in all the pads, in general, appearing smaller in the track than they actually are.

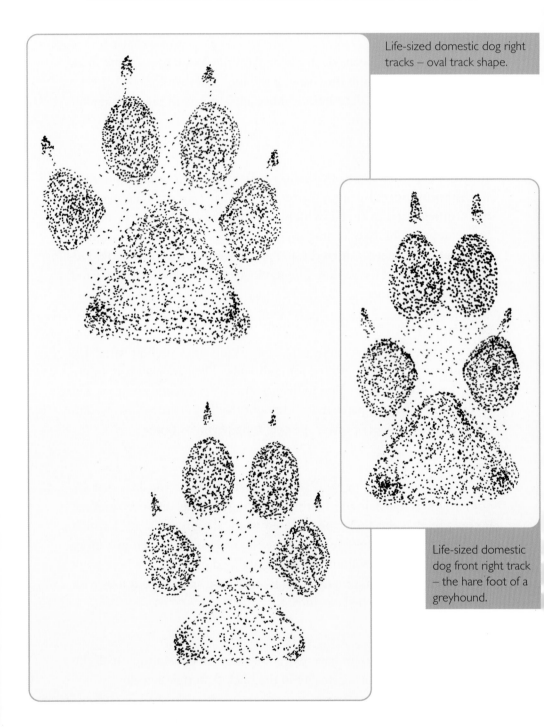

Life-sized domestic dog right tracks – oval track shape.

Life-sized domestic dog front right track – the hare foot of a greyhound.

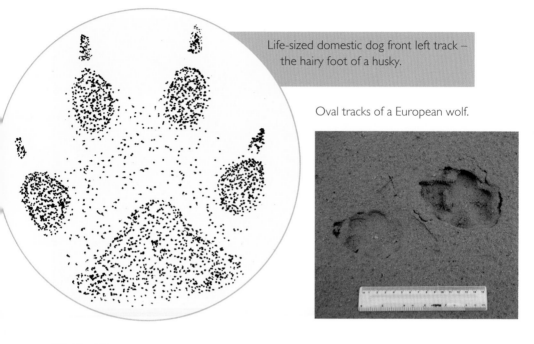

Life-sized domestic dog front left track – the hairy foot of a husky.

Oval tracks of a European wolf.

Webbed Foot

I have not yet managed to see evidence of webbing in the track of a dog but theoretically it is possible with breeds such as the Newfoundland, which do have at least partially webbed feet and presumably show this feature in their tracks.

I had considerable help from Linda Bittle with these dog types, which may on the surface seem a little academic. However, she correctly pointed out to me that as wildlife trackers we may become involved in solving cases of wildlife crime or livestock worrying. Being able to identify the culprit, even in broad terms, may be very useful.

Below left: Domestic dog, cat-footed arrangement.

Below right: Note the canid triangular outer toes on both the front and rear tracks.

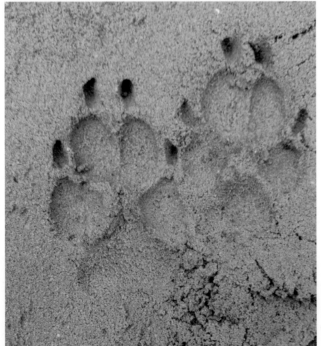

Above: Husky tracks.

Left: Hare-footed domestic dog tracks. (RA)

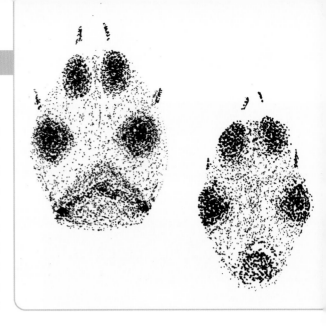

RED FOX

Red foxes differ from dogs mostly because of their hairy feet. Naked pads are needed to pick up soil or make an impression in average substrate, and therefore red fox toes and interdigital pads appear tiny in comparison to the overall track, although the general shapes are very similar to those of dogs.

The interdigital pad on the front track of a fox most frequently shows as a bar or chevron, whereas on the rear track it looks like a dot or occasionally a small bar; so much so that in an obscured rear track print the interdigital pad can sometimes be confused with one of the toes. Claws also differ in that foxes are more cat-like and very regularly do not show in the track at all.

Above left: Perfect red fox tracks. The rear track is ahead of the front, to the right of the photo.

Above right: An understep walk of a red fox.

Right: Although partially obscured, the triangular outer toes give this away as a red fox.

The direct-registered trot of a European wolf. See the section on gaits and track patterns.

Red Fox Versus Dog

I look for the following features to test the difference between fox and dog tracks. Some of these have already been stated but, for me, in order of reliability, I look for the following. The small bar or chevron-shaped interdigital on the fox front track, and a dot on the rear; tiny toes; the presence of hair registering in the substrate; drawing an x-shape across the negative space which should pass through the track without cutting across any pads in the fox. Many people will use the top edge of toes two and five as a guide – where an imaginary line drawn between these points that doesn't hit the bottom of toes three and four is indicative of a fox. Keep in mind, though, that this is also the case with hare-footed dogs.

Size is a great help, as even a large fox will not leave a track much bigger than that of a Jack Russell terrier or a small whippet.

Gait: Dogs and foxes both commonly trot and foxes, especially, often direct register when they trot, as do many wild canids.

Species	Rear L x W (cm) +/ −	Front L x W (cm) +/ −
Domestic dog (*Canis lupus familiaris*)	Extremely variable	Extremely variable
Red fox (*Vulpes vulpes*)	4.5 x 3.2	4.5 x 3.5

UNGULIGRADES

This large group is represented in our region by domestic animals (including cows, horses and sheep), wild animals (deer and wild boar) and feral and escaped animals (such as goats). There may be exotics found too, especially llamas and alpacas, with the increasing interest in walking with these animals in the countryside and their tracks therefore being found a long way from obvious farms and small holdings. Many sheep farmers also use them for protection within their flocks as they are known to be aggressive towards dogs.

Cows and horses are increasingly being used for conservation grazing, and often the smaller varieties such as Dartmoor and Koenig ponies and Belted Galloways and Highland cows. It is possible to confuse these cows and horses with each other and with our native red deer.

ODD-TOED UNGULATES – PERISSODACTYLA

In the UK, we have only horses representing this group of mammals.

HORSES AND PONIES

Horses and ponies stand on a complicated arrangement of toes that seem to be fused into or becoming part of toe three. They have a toe pad, known as the frog, which reaches deep into the track, and begins outside the arc created by the hoof wall. The frog is not always visible, especially on hard substrates and on horses with shod feet. I do see it regularly in shod tracks and assume that it is most evident when the shoe is worn. Unshod (or natural) tracks, like the one illustrated in the drawing, show the frog much more reliably.

The hoof wall can show as an almost complete circle, especially on the front feet. Frequently, the rears are more pinched and can therefore appear longer than they are wide. Very often they are smaller than the fronts.

Gait: Horses tend to walk and trot. Even ridden horses don't necessarily get galloped as much as you might imagine.

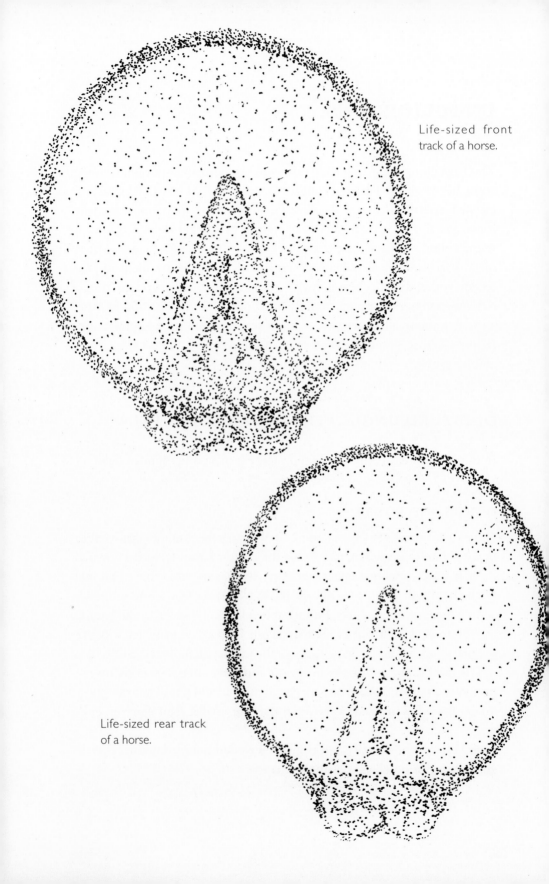

Life-sized front
track of a horse.

Life-sized rear track
of a horse.

Above left: Front and rear of shod horse.

Above right: Sometimes all that is seen of a horse track is the dig caused by the front of the shoe.

Right: Slightly more obscure, but the frog helps here with identification.

EVEN-TOED UNGULATES – ARTIODACTYL

Aside from horses, all of our other ungulates fall into this category and have two cleats on each of their four feet. If there is a difference in the length of the cleats, then the shortest cleat is always on the inside of the track. These are, in reality, toes three and four, with the latter being the longest. Toes two and five exist as dew claws higher up the leg.

COWS

The feet of cattle are fully divided into two cleats that are fully rounded along the whole outside edge of the hoof wall. They also have dew claws, but these are set quite high up the leg and tend to register only in the deepest substrate. The toe pads extend to approximately one third of the length of the cleats. Front tracks are usually larger than the rear.

Frequently, as with horses, location can be a good clue when identifying cow tracks, but conservation grazing animals are used in all kinds of remote

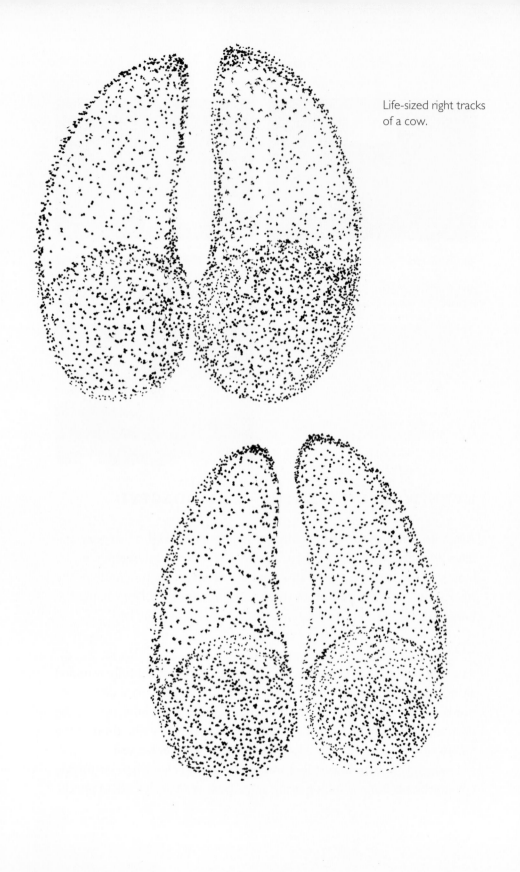

Life-sized right tracks of a cow.

areas, and animals can escape and roam. I once tracked and recovered a small group of six Belted Galloway cows that had escaped from a downland grazing project and travelled 3–4km into adjacent woods. When they entered the woods and started to move across dry leaf litter, their tracks were surprisingly hard to see, or hard to see as cow tracks rather than a large deer or pony.

Gait: Cows almost always walk.

Horse Versus Cow Versus Red Deer

On good substrate you would think these animals could not be mistaken. However, it happens regularly, and I have seen it a number of times during evaluations where people mis-identify partial horse tracks as cows. It is also possible to confuse ponies and colts with red deer, especially if the tracks are partial. Such mistakes are usually due to the tracker focusing on the frog (as described above), and in some tracks it isn't always obvious where this starts and finishes, so it can give the impression of a cloven foot. Check this carefully, and in softer substrates also check for dew claws, which both cows and deer have.

In some circumstances, the floor of the track can be a real mess and picking out the cloven feet of cows especially is difficult. Often location is the key, but this can also throw out your reasoning. On a track and sign evaluation a few years back, some cows had entered a small woodland, probably a week or two before, and next to this woodland was a field with horses in. Almost everyone in the group put two and two together to equal horse, missing the clear dew claws evident in the track I questioned them about.

Above left: Cow tracks.
Above right: Cow tracks can be surprisingly obscure and hard to identify.

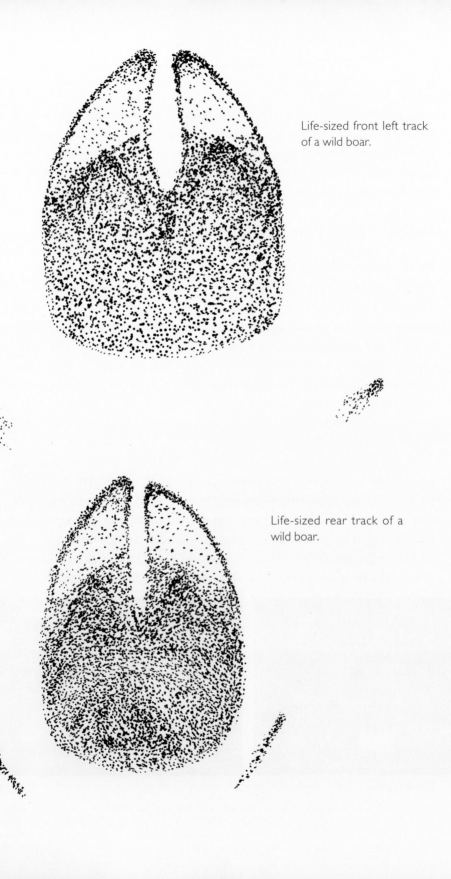

Life-sized front left track
of a wild boar.

Life-sized rear track of a
wild boar.

WILD BOAR

The tracks of wild boar are easy to identify in good substrate. They have well-rounded hoof walls, especially towards the tip. The cleats are joined at the proximal edge and this shows as a blocky compression shape taking up approximately half the length of the track. This shape is, in fact, the two fused toe pads.

The negative space between the two cleats is normally wide and frequently the two edges are not parallel to each other. Dew claws will almost always show if the ground is soft, but do not rely solely on this (pun intended). It is more accurate to say that in wild boar, and pigs in general, the dew claws almost always touch the ground, but they don't always leave a mark. Unlike all of our deer species, the dew claws, if showing, will always be outside the lines of the cleats. They are bigger and more pronounced on the front track and thinner, longer and placed closer to the hoof on the rear. The most likely confusion animal would be with tracks of a red deer.

Gait: Wild boar tend to walk and trot.

Left: Wild Boar track showing the fused, long toe pads.

Right: Wild Boar piglets.

95

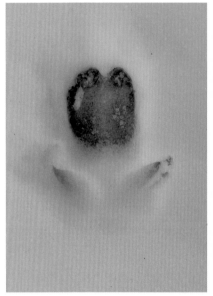 

Left: Registered wild boar track in the snow.

Right: A partial register on a wild boar track showing the blunt tips and curved outer hoof wall. (RN)

DEER

We have six species of deer in the UK, seven if we also include some semi-feral herds of reindeer in Scotland. Only the red and the roe are actually native.

Three species, the red, sika and fallow deer, produce quite large antlers and so the males have significantly larger front feet than rear. This is an adaptation to help support the weight of the antlers and the associated thick-set necks and broader shoulders that are needed as they clash antlers during the rut. By comparison, roe deer have small antlers which are not really used in combat and so the relative size of front and rear tracks is not a reliable way of sexing them. This is true also of Reeves's muntjac deer, with its tiny antlers, and Chinese water deer, which have no antlers at all.

When identifying deer tracks, pay particular attention to the presence and absence of the toe pads, and how far these pads extend into the track. On hard substrates, the toe pads, even if normally present, may not register, making identification harder. When they do show, they give the floor of the track a bump where the edge of the pad meets the subunguis. Also, pay particular attention to the shape of the outside edge of the hoof wall. As with the other ungulates already described, if there is a difference in lengths of the cleats then the inside cleat is shorter and often narrower. The hoof wall starts from the distal end of the toe pad, which can also help when trying to establish how long the toe pad actually is.

The front tracks of all deer species can splay much further apart than the rear tracks, which they do when moving fast or across soft substrates. Dew claws, toes two and five, may also show in these circumstances. In the front tracks, the dew claws will often appear as slightly longer and sticking out to the sides more than in the rear tracks, where they register more like dots directly behind the cleats.

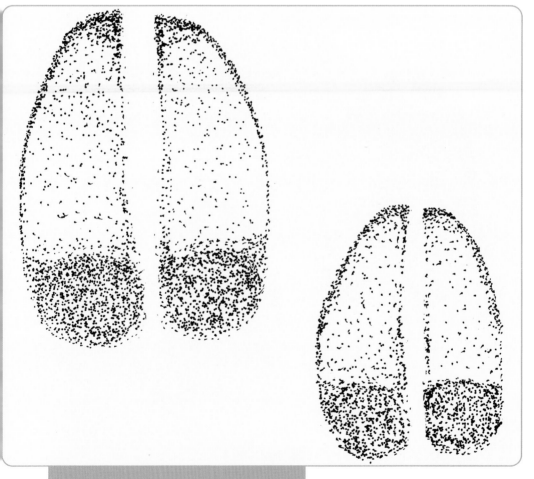

Life-sized left tracks of a red deer.

Life-sized left foot track of a red deer with a more rounded hoof wall.

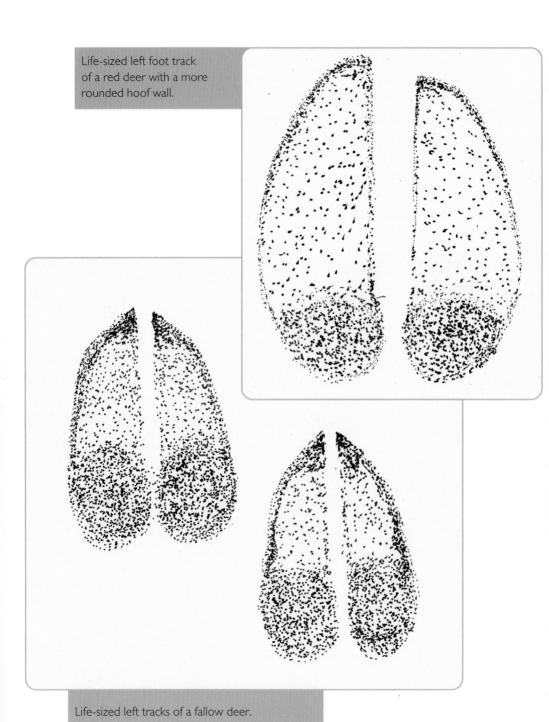

Life-sized left tracks of a fallow deer.

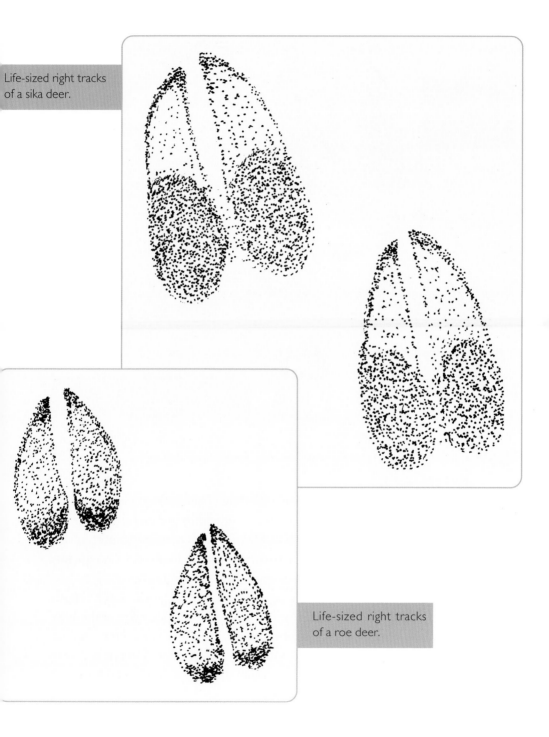

Life-sized right tracks of a sika deer.

Life-sized right tracks of a roe deer.

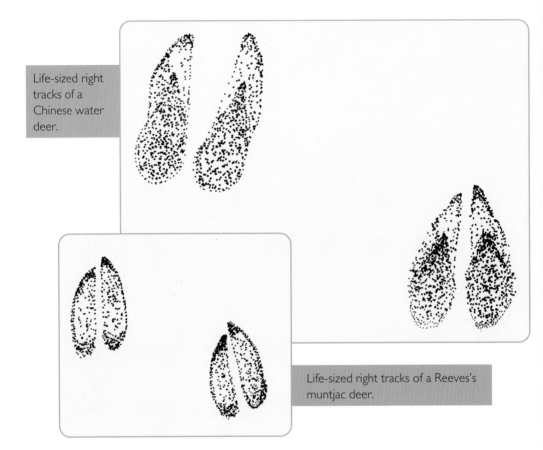

Life-sized right tracks of a Chinese water deer.

Life-sized right tracks of a Reeves's muntjac deer.

Red Deer

Red deer are our largest truly wild native land mammal, but their size varies considerably, depending on where in the UK they are found. Deer living in the relatively impoverished Scottish Highlands are significantly smaller than those living it up in the royal parks in southern England. Consequently, their tracks will vary considerably in size from region to region.

The toe pads generally take up about a quarter of the track length, perhaps slightly more on the rear track, and the outside edge of the hoof wall can be straight, giving it a boxy appearance. But this often presents as being quite rounded. In the south of England, where I live, it is easy to identify these animals by the sheer size of their tracks, once, of course, you have decided it is a deer of some kind.

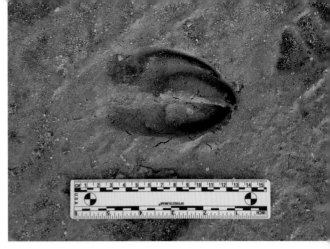

Above left: Red deer tracks showing the extreme difference between the rear and front tracks, indicating a stag.

Above right: Note the distance the toe pads extend into the track on this red deer stag.

Left: Red deer tracks can look enormous, especially when they splay during fast movement.

Red Deer Versus Wild Boar

Wild boar will probably be the most likely confusion species when considering red deer, especially with partial tracks or those on difficult substrates, especially on leaf litter. In these situations, sometimes following a particular trail for a while is the only way to be sure. Wild boar trails often go into places where red deer cannot venture, or into places with obvious wild boar sign like rooting, distinctive beds and rubbed trees.

In better substrates, check the curve on the outside hoof, which in wild boar is much more rounded, especially in the top third or so, but do keep in mind that some red deer tracks are curved too. Also check the very tip of the cleat. In wild boar, the point where the inside hoof wall and the outside meet is wider giving a blunter appearance. If you can see the toe pads and dew claws, these are very reliable indicators.

Red Deer Versus Cows and Horses

This is another possible area of confusion, so check carefully the features described above in the section on 'Horses Versus Cows Versus Red Deer'.

Fallow Deer

Generally speaking, fallow deer tracks are fairly consistent, with the majority of individuals showing the outsides of the hoof wall as relatively straight and bending in quite close to the tip. They are most likely to be confused with sika or red deer.

As well as being straight, the hoof walls converge towards the centre of the track from the point where they leave the toe pads. In other words, the outer hoof walls are not parallel to each other. Fallow deer toe pads cover around a third of the track length. To my eyes, the overall track shape gives the impression of a church window.

Above left: Straight hoof walls angling in from the ends of the toe pad are features to look for with fallow deer tracks. Note also how the hoof wall angles into the tip, very close to the end of the track.

Above right: A fallow deer track in leaf litter. If you would like to follow animals, it is important to recognise tracks in the most difficult of substrates.

Right: Multiple fallow deer tracks.

Below: Fallow deer track, partially registered rear on front in hard substrate.

Above left: Rear and front sika deer tracks.

Above right: Note how far the toe pad extends into this sika deer track.

Sika Deer

The tracks of sika deer are, in my experience, much more variable amongst individuals than those of fallow deer. All of my sika deer track photographs were taken in a woodland in southern Ireland, where they are the only large species of deer present, so there was no possibility of misidentification. The toe pads can be key to identification as they make up almost half of the overall track length.

Fallow Versus Red Versus Sika Deer

I have alluded to the main differences in the text above, but to summarise, the tracker should focus on the shape of the hoof wall and the proportional length of the toe pad.

The fallow deer toe pad is around a third of the track length, and the hoof walls are straight but lean into the track with the tip forming late on. Sika deer have a longer toe pad, almost half the length of the track, and they appear more rounded than fallow tracks. Red deer toe pads are short at around a quarter of the track length. The hoof walls, even when they curve, appear to run parallel to the centre of the track for longer.

Roe Deer

Unlike the deer described so far, the roe deer toe pads rarely register in the track. When they do, it is not usually a 'fingerprint' but tends to show as more of a smudge at the extreme proximal end of the track, and only then if the substrate is soft. This means that the floor of the track is flat along its length, without the classic bump that the species so far described show. In soft substrates, it may present as small bump or step but not to the same degree as the bigger species.

The hoof wall begins to curve in towards the tip immediately, which results in a characteristic heart-shaped footprint which is further enhanced by the sharp points to the tips of the cleats. In soft substrates including sand, roe deer tracks can, however, appear boxy, so be sure to check all the features.

Below left: A classic roe deer track.

Below right: Even in this loose substrate, the heart-shaped rear roe deer track on the right is visible.

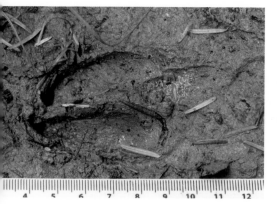

Below left: Heart-shaped roe deer tracks with rear on top of front.

Below right: All deer tracks, including roe, can look a little blocky in deep substrates. Look closely at the track on the right to spot the roe deer features.

Above left: Note the large toe pads on these Chinese water deer feet. On both the fronts (left) and rear (right) these extend well into the cleat. Note also the dew claws, toes two and five, that all deer have, and the size difference between front and rear.

Above right: Slight overstep of the rear foot on top of the front in these Chinese water deer tracks.

Above left: Chinese water deer front tracks seem to splay extensively, even for deer.

Above right: Chinese water deer rear and front tracks.

Left: Note the large front track splay, even at relatively slow speeds.

Chinese Water Deer

These animals are confined to fairly specific parts of the country and so can be eliminated in many regions when trying to accurately identify one of our smaller deer species. Their tracks can be of a similar size to roe deer but are characterised by the large amount of toe pad that shows. In fact, almost all of the cleat seems to be made up of the pads, which certainly extend beyond halfway along its length. In addition to the large toe pads, the front tracks splay significantly, even at relatively slow gaits, and certainly more than any other small deer at these slow speeds.

Reeves's Muntjac Deer

These are our smallest deer and correspondingly produce the smallest tracks. It is possible to confuse the footprints with roe deer, especially in registered tracks or with some slippage making the tracks appear relatively large. Like roe deer tracks, the toe pad does not present significantly even in very clear muntjac tracks. The outside edge of the hoof wall is straight, and although this is possible with all deer species, the inside cleat is almost always noticeably shorter.

Above left: Registered track of Reeves's muntjac, showing rear on top of front. Note the straight hoof walls and the uneven cleat length making this a right foot.

Above right: With more energy as the front tracks are splayed, but still showing identifiable Reeves's muntjac features.

Muntjac Versus Roe Deer

Look in the floor of the track to make sure you are seeing the true size of the track. The most likely area of confusion is with young roe deer, which are only of a similar size for a short period in the spring and early summer. But even young roe deer will exhibit the curved, heart-shaped outer wall of the hoof.

GOATS AND SHEEP

Sheep

Sheep can vary enormously in size but some of the smaller breeds, and of course lambs, can leave tracks that resemble those of deer, especially roe deer. Toe pads generally extend to around a quarter of the track length with the outer edges of the hoof walls relatively straight. Sheep tend toward blunt tips to their cleats which can help separate them from roe deer.

Goats

Like sheep, goats can vary significantly in size, from pygmy goats upwards. The toe pads extend to almost a third of the track length. The outer hoof wall is more arched than in sheep tracks, and the inner hoof walls are not parallel to each other. The tips of the cleats are blunt compared with deer and may even appear hooked.

Life-sized left tracks of sheep.

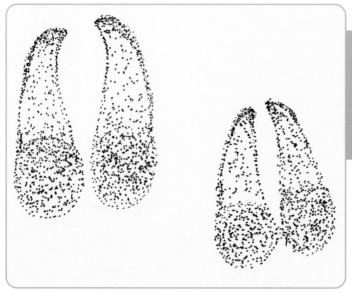

Life-sized right tracks of goat.

Above left: Front left track of sheep.

Above right: Front and rear sheep tracks.

Right: Typical blunted sheep track complete with scats.

Above left: Goat's rear right foot registered on top of front. (TB)

Above right: Hind left track of a feral goat. (TB)

Roe Deer Versus Sheep and Goats

I believe that sheep are most likely to be confused with roe deer as they are often found in the same areas, can be of a similar size, and also have a toe pad that doesn't extend very far into the track. Check especially for straight sides to the outside of the hoof wall and the broad and therefore bluntly rounded cleat tips in sheep. Also check the differences described above between goats and sheep.

Gait: All deer, sheep and goats tend to walk and trot.

Species	Rear L x W (cm) +/ −	Front L x W (cm) +/ −
Horse (*Equus caballus*)	Extremely variable	Extremely variable
Cow (*Bos taurus*)	Extremely variable	Extremely variable
Wild boar (*Sus scrofa*)	9.6 x 7.0	8.5 x 6.5
Red deer (*Cervus elaphus*)	7.0 x 5.0	8.5 x 6.8
Fallow deer (*Dama dama*)	6.2 x 4.2	6.5 x 4.4
Sika deer (*Cervus nippon*)	6.4 x 4.0	6.4 x 4.4
Roe deer (*Capreolus capreolus*)	4.0 x 2.7	4.0 x 3.0
Chinese water deer (*Hydropotes inermis*)	3.8 x 2.6	4.0 x 3.4
Reeves's muntjac deer (*Muntiacus reevesi*)	2.2 x 1.5	2.5 x 1.5
Feral goat (*Capra hircus*)	Extremely variable	Extremely variable
Sheep (*Ovis aries*)	Extremely variable	Extremely variable

EXOTICS

There are a few animals on the loose in the UK that may not immediately spring to mind when out tracking, so I have outlined those that are most likely to be encountered, and those which may become widespread if they are not controlled.

ALPACA, LLAMA AND THE LIKE

These animals are closely related to camels and have cloven feet that are fused for approximately a third of the length of the foot (from the proximal end). What shows in the track is all toe pad for most of the track length, until the end, which has relatively small nails.

RED-NECKED WALLABY

Colonies of red-necked wallaby in the UK are very localised, but where they do occur it will be the rear tracks that are most frequently encountered. Most often, it is a long, tapering finger with a bulbous pad at the proximal end that is seen, with a smaller 'finger' off this, pointing to the

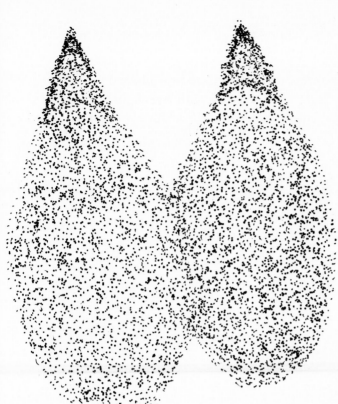

Life-sized right front track
of an alpaca.

Life-sized right rear
track of an alpaca.

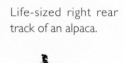

Alpaca tracks, with the front track
at the top of the photo.

outside of the trail. This makes up the common two-pronged impression of wallaby tracks. The fronts are hand-like with five digits and a large interdigital pad. Toe one registers weakly or not at all.

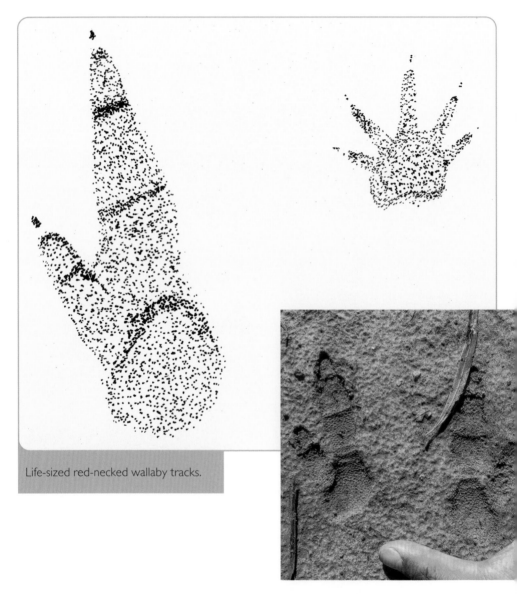

Life-sized red-necked wallaby tracks.

Red-necked wallaby rear tracks. (CP)

RACCOON

This species has been spotted in a few locations; probably escaped individuals, although there may be a small colony in England. Their tracks are very distinctive, looking like tiny hands. The heel of the rear track may show consistently, but the key feature is the long digits, which will register for their full length and therefore appear as if joined to the interdigital pad. This pad looks a like a giant kidney bean in shape. Raccoons have five toes on both front and rear feet.

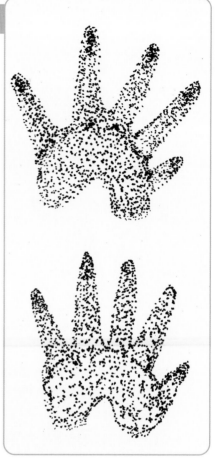

Raccoon tracks.

RACCOON DOG

This is a strange creature, whose tracks are very similar to those of domestic dogs. They are completely unrelated but have very similar tracks, which can be confused with both dog and possibly fox, and they have dog-sized toes. The front track especially has a very wide spread, relative to its size, and this makes toes two and five appear to be pointing outwards more than with a dog. These same toes are also less triangular than with canines. Toes three and four fuse low down and this may be evident in the track. These two toes are also very large compared with toes two and five, especially on the front feet. The rear tracks have similar features but are slightly smaller overall.

Life-sized right tracks of a raccoon dog.

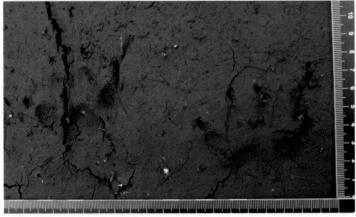

Raccoon dog front and rear tracks. (SR)

Species	Rear L x W (cm) +/ −	Front L x W (cm) +/ −
Alpaca (*Vicugna pacos*)	10 x 8.0	10.5 x 9.0
Red-necked wallaby (*Macropus rufogriseus*)	10.5 x 5.0	3.8 x 3.8
Raccoon (*Procyon lotor*)	5.0 x 4.0	5.5 x 5.4
Raccoon dog (*Nytereutes procyonoides*)	3.6 x 3.0	3.5 x 4.0

GAITS AND TRACK PATTERNS

Animals generally have a standard way in which they prefer to move – or put another way, all things being equal, any particular individual will choose to walk, trot or bound and so on during the normal course of its normal day. This standard way of moving is often referred to as the baseline gait. It's easy to witness this for yourself with domestic animals. Dogs, for example, and canines in general, like to trot. They spend most of their time happily doing this, hoping to come across tantalising smells that may lead them to a meal or a mate, or anything else that takes their fancy. Deer, on the other hand, tend to walk everywhere.

For the tracker, understanding how an animal is moving – in other words its gait – and the pattern that gait leaves on the ground in the arrangement of the tracks, gives clues as to how the animal is reacting to its environment and, crucially, you, the tracker. Should an animal such as a dog suddenly slow down from a trot to a walk, there will be a reason for this. Should a deer change from a walk to a trot or an even faster gait, there will also be a reason for this. If you happen to be following this animal, the reason for this change in gait might be that it has become aware of your presence. In this situation, the best thing the tracker can do is wait for a time, allow the animal to settle, and then carry on following. Understanding how the animal is moving across the landscape connects the tracker much more closely with both the animal and the landscape.

Basic gaits, and the resulting track patterns, can be broken down into four types: walk, trot, lope or canter, and gallop. There are a couple of other variations – bounding and hopping – which tend to be used by specific animals or in specific circumstances and will be explained later.

These first four basic gaits can also be broken down into two sub-categories: those that leave regular-spaced patterns on the ground and those that leave irregular patterns on the ground.

Before discussing these gaits, it is useful to introduce some basic terminology.

- **Stride** is the distance between the track made by one foot, to the point that same foot is seen again.

- **Half stride** is the point between the foot on one side of the body to the corresponding foot on the other side of the body. For example, left rear to right rear.

- **Straddle** is the width of the trail, measured from the extreme edge of the tracks on each side of the body.

- **Median line** is an imaginary line running down through the centre of the trail.

- **Track group** refers to a grouping of tracks on the trail in faster gaits. With these movements, all four feet may be visible as separate feet, thus forming a group of four.

- **Inter-group distance** is the distance between the track groups as described above.

TRACK PATTERNS WITH EVEN SPACING

Even-spaced track patterns are those that show a regularity in the strides and half strides, which happens when an animal is walking or trotting. This really applies to four-legged mammals in which the front and rear legs are roughly the same length. Throughout these movement patterns, the distance between the tracks remains constant, to the point where it would be easily measurable. If, for example, the stride is 80cm and the half stride 40cm, these distances remain more or less constant until the animal changes the way it moves. There are various types of walks and trots, which relate to varying speeds, and these can be useful to understand to get a clear idea of how the animal is moving.

TYPES OF WALK

When an animal walks it is always in contact with the ground, and mostly with three legs touching at any one time. For example, as the animal moves forwards it will lift its rear leg, let's say the right rear, which lands somewhere close to the right front. This sequence is then repeated on the other side of the body. The front foot may lift off just before the rear lands, which can allow the rear foot to land on top of the track left by the front. This is called a direct register. If it is partly on top, it is an indirect or partial register.

The rear foot landing ahead of the front track is an overstep walk, and landing behind the front track is an understep walk. In general, the further forward the rear tracks land in relation to the front, the faster the animal is moving. In this scenario, the overstep walk is likely to be faster than a direct register walk, which is likely to be faster than an understep walk. Sometimes an understep walk is a stalking gait, as the rear foot touches down before the front lifts off, leaving no space for the rear because the front has not yet moved.

Walks are identifiable by the relatively short stride and the relatively wide straddle, and can be helpful in identifying the animal involved. This is particularly useful when trailing, and especially where the substrate is such that it is difficult to identify the animal accurately. For example, on grass and leaf litter, indistinct compression shapes may be all that can be seen.

American naturalist and tracker James Halfpenny discovered that on an animal walking (and it must be walking) with even-length legs, the stride is roughly equivalent to the distance between the hips and shoulders of the animal. I have used this to good effect when trying to identify between various deer species I have been trailing. It can even be used if only a half stride can be seen by doubling this distance to arrive at the length of the full stride.

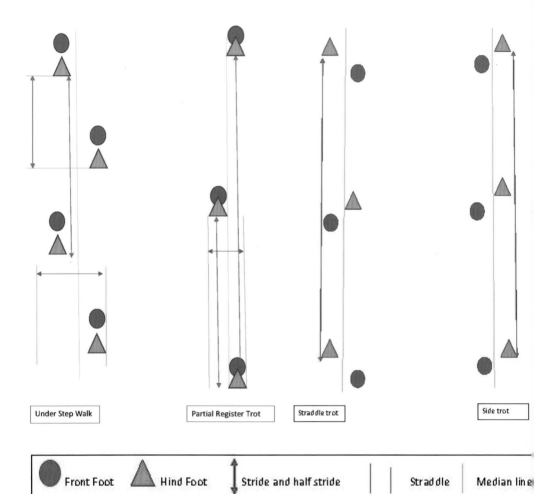

Under Step Walk	Partial Register Trot	Straddle trot	Side trot

Front Foot	Hind Foot	Stride and half stride	Straddle	Median line

TROTS

Trots are different to walks in the way the animal is moving but are similar in the track pattern left on the ground. In a trot, the animals move with diagonal opposite limbs airborne and landing simultaneously, left rear and right front for example. In the same way as for walks, trots can be understep, overstep, direct register or partial register. And as with walks, the faster the trot, the further ahead of the front tracks the rears will land.

There is a limit to how far an animal can throw its rear feet forwards before it kicks its own front legs, and so, to avoid this, some animals have developed a couple of other gait strategies – the straddle trot and side trot. The straddle trot is where the rear legs swing forward outside of the fronts, and so land ahead of them and on the outer edge of the trail. A side trot is where the animal skews its body to place all the rear feet on one side of the median line and the fronts on the other. You may have seen this with domestic dogs that appear to be facing to one side but still moving forwards.

The characteristics of trots are a longer stride length and a narrower straddle – so narrow, in fact, that the tracks may appear to be on the median line. Working out the animal's hip to shoulder length from its stride is less accurate when it is moving in a trot. It may be that the stride length in a trot represents one and half to two times the hip to shoulder length.

In both trots and walks, the rear foot is likely to land on top of the front track, so be aware of this when trying to identify the animal that left the tracks, as you may be looking at more than one foot in each track, which can distort the shapes quite significantly.

A direct-register walk of a Reeves's muntjac.

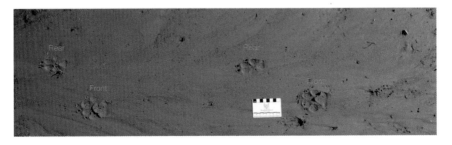

Side trot in a domestic dog.

 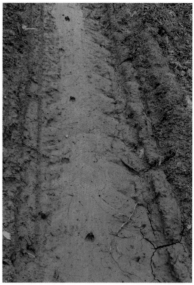

Above left: Overstep walk in a domestic dog.

Above right: Roe deer in a direct-register trot. The straddle is narrow, and the stride is long.

PATTERNS WITH UNEVEN SPACING

With walks and trots, the animal moves with its back flat and its legs relatively straight. Faster gaits – lopes and gallops – involve a 'bunching in' at the waist as the back legs reach further forwards. The animal is airborne during both of these gaits, at least once in the cycle of footfall with lopes and twice in the case of gallops. Feet land independently and, in most cases, make individual marks on the ground. However, it is possible with rotary lopes and gallops, explained below, for the track group, which is normally all four feet, to appear to be made up of three feet as one of the rears registers on top of the front track.

These gaits, unlike walks and trots, leave uneven track patterns, although this may not be immediately obvious, so it is good practice to check a couple of things to be sure you're looking at a faster gait. Direct register trots can some–

times look like a faster movement but, in these cases, each mark on the ground is made by both front and rear. Fast track patterns, even if they look regularly spaced, and in a line like a trot, are individual feet. Closer inspection in these cases will almost always reveal a difference in the distances between the four feet and certainly in the inter-group spacing. As with other gaits, the faster the animal is moving, the further ahead the rear feet land in front of its front feet.

It is difficult to distinguish fast lopes from slow gallops, although if both rear feet land ahead of both fronts it is most likely a gallop. Both lopes and gallops can be either rotary or transverse depending on the sequence in which the feet land, leaving subtly different track patterns.

The diagrams below illustrate the sequence of foot falls in both fast gaits. The sequence can start from either side of the body, but I have illustrated the sequence starting with the left front foot.

There are variations of lopes, in particular, where the sequence of foot falls remains the same but the rear feet may land directly on top of the front feet. This is often called a 2 x 2 lope due to the paired marks left on the ground. Sometimes only one front foot is covered or partially covered by a rear foot, thus leaving three marks on the ground in a gait termed a 3 x 4 lope. They fall into the lope category because the sequence of foot falls is the same as a conventional lope, but the sets of tracks land very close together and are not normally strung out. They can be both traverse or rotary and are commonly used by mustelids (the weasel family), rodents and shrews. These are creatures that concertina their bodies as they move, which leads to the close foot placement.

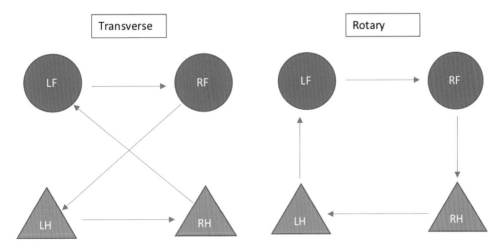

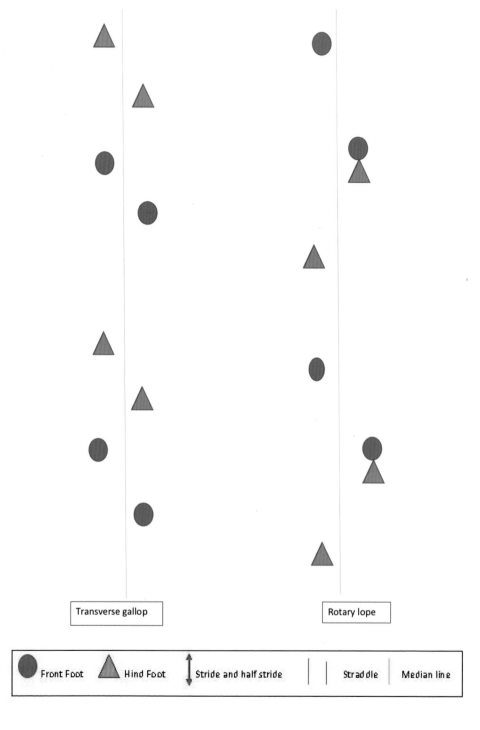

Transverse gallop

Rotary lope

Front Foot | Hind Foot | Stride and half stride | Straddle | Median line

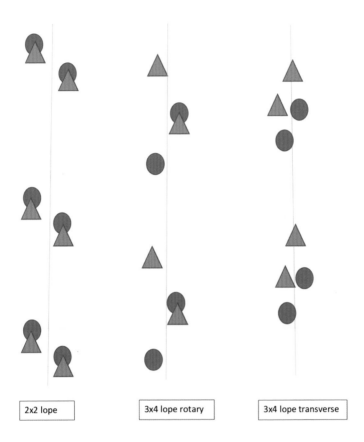

| 2x2 lope | 3x4 lope rotary | 3x4 lope transverse |

Bounding and hopping gaits differ from both the slow and fast gaits mentioned so far because the rear feet land and leave the ground almost simultaneously, in something like a series of jumps. The rear feet, in this instance, are often side by side, or very close to this. The main difference between a hop and a bound is where in relation to the front feet the rear feet land. In hops, they land behind the front feet and in bounds, the rear feet swing past the front feet to land beyond. Rabbits and squirrels move this way, as a matter of course, but other species including rodents may also use this gait even if only on certain substrates.

Another reasonably common gait, used especially by deer, is pronking or stotting. In this movement, the animal leaves the ground and lands on all four feet simultaneously. This is often used in response to the presence of a predator and is thought to demonstrate fitness to a watching carnivore.

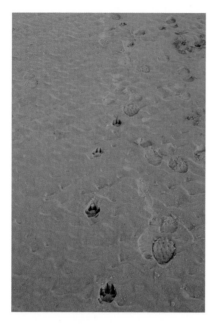

Above: This dog is moving at top speed in a rotary gallop, with both smaller rear tracks landing beyond the larger fronts. The dew claw, toe one, is also visible, suggesting energy in the movement.

Below: A transverse gallop set of four tracks with both rear tracks ahead of the fronts.

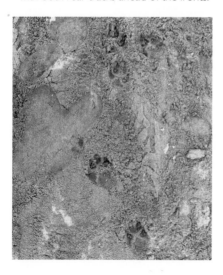

Weasel on ink in the classic mustelid lope.

Rabbit trail moving away from the camera showing rear tracks overtaking the fronts.

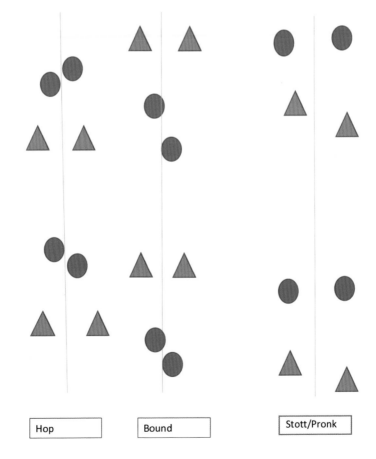

Hop   Bound   Stott/Pronk

BIRD TRACKS

This section covering bird tracks is a little more generic than the preceding section on mammal tracks. I intend it as an introduction to what will eventually, I am sure, turn into a much bigger and more elaborate body of work. I have covered in some detail the major distinctions in identifying bird tracks to groups and, where possible, to species. However, it could be that with some groups this guide will only get you as far as, for example, small gull, medium-sized gull and large gull.

There are many species, however, whose identity is easily confirmed through tracks. I have only included common birds of this region and, perhaps more importantly, those that regularly land on the ground and actually leave tracks.

Tracking should be about finding animals, or at least determining their presence. Because many bird species spend very little time on the ground, or are extremely light-footed, there are better ways of assessing their presence than through tracking. The best trackers are also well-rounded naturalists and learning to identify birds, both visually and through their calls, is a must. For example, when trailing, a knowledge of bird alarms becomes essential. A bird's alarm call may well alert you to the presence of your quarry – or indeed alert your quarry to your presence. With the mammals of this region, it is possible to identify almost all of our species by their tracks, given good-quality footprints. This is much harder with birds. Having said that, I do believe that with further study it will be possible to identify many more birds to the species level than I imply now.

FOOT MORPHOLOGY

Birds are different to mammals in that toe five, the little finger, is absent. Toe one, or the thumb, may not always show in many groups of birds, so it may appear that the bird has only three toes. Regardless of how many toes are showing, they all converge in the central metatarsal space.

Birds walk with their weight focused on the ends of the toes and are all therefore digitigrades. The various arrangements of the toes on a bird's foot have been classified thoroughly and I include the basic categories below.

CLASSIC BIRD TRACKS

Should a child be asked to draw a bird track it is likely that their track would have three toes facing forwards and one back. This 'classic' track is properly termed anisodactyl, with the three toes facing forwards being toes two, three and four. Toe one – the thumb, or hallux – is facing back. These classic bird feet belong, amongst others, to our passerines, or perching birds. Imagine these birds sitting on a branch with the hallux wrapping under and around that branch to keep them from falling off. There are many birds in this group with this foot structure.

GAME BIRDS AND WADING BIRDS

These are the birds that really spend a great deal of time on the ground. They also have the anisodactyl foot structure, but the hallux is occasionally missing or greatly reduced and therefore may not show in the track, show weakly, or only occasionally show. Many of the wading birds may also have at least partial webbing between some of the toes.

WEB-FOOTED BIRDS

These birds represent a variation on the game bird/wader track, which in addition to being anisodactyl also have varying amounts of full-length webbing between the toes. This webbing may be close to the metatarsal area and only extend partway out along the toes in what is termed a semi–palmate foot. If the webbing extends more or less to the ends of the toes, it is referred to as palmate. In both of these foot types, the webbing is only present between toes two, three and four. However, a small number of bird species have full-length webbing between all four toes and are termed totipalmate. A variant on the general webbing theme is termed lobate, where the individual toes have extra fleshy fringes.

ZYGODACTYL BIRDS

The final foot type commonly encountered in our region is for birds that have all four toes of a substantial length, but with two facing forwards and two back in a structure termed zygodactyl. For some birds, this is more or less a permeant arrangement, while others can alternate, with three forwards and one back, should they choose, and then switch back to the zygodactyl arrangement as needed.

Above, left to right:

Classic bird track of the blackbird. Note the bulbous toe pads on toes one and three.
Zygodactyl foot of the green woodpecker.
Jackdaw foot. Note the hugging inner toe.
Totipalmate foot of a cormorant.
Tawny owl foot.
Classic game bird foot of a pheasant.

TRACK GROUPS

When identifying birds from their tracks there are various features to look closely at, including the distances between toes; the relative lengths of the toes; and the angles the toes radiate from the central metatarsal space (which will make the track more or less symmetrical). It is also good to check for webbing, which may be full, partial or only between certain toes. Claws may also be long or short, and the metatarsal area may be of a significant size or shape, or show prominently or not at all. This metatarsal area can be treated in the same way as negative space in mammal tracks.

For the birds described below, I have arranged them in groups that seem to make sense with regards to their foot structure. This could be because they live in similar habitats and therefore have similar evolutionary adaptations, or that they are closely related.

MEASURING BIRD TRACKS

I have included measurements for the species described. I do not include claws in these measurement as often they do not show in the tracks. For track length, birds with an absent or reduced hallux are measured

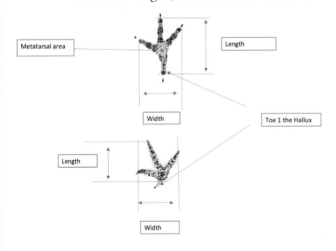

from the back of the metatarsal area to the tip of the leading toe, number three. Classic bird tracks are measured from the end of the toe pads on the leading toe three, to the end of the toe pad on the hallux. In all cases, width is measured from the extreme extent of the outer toes, excluding any claws.

This illustration (see previous page) shows the right track of a buzzard and the right track of a grouse, showing how both classic and game bird tracks are measured.

WATER BIRDS

I have chosen to include four regularly encountered birds here, which are most frequently found around water margins or in wet meadows. The birds described below have classic anisodactyl foot structure.

HERONS AND EGRETS

Herons and Egrets are in the same family and their foot morphology is very similar. In fact, throughout the world the feet of the species in this family look the same. They show the classic bird track of three toes pointing forwards, with a long hallux pointing backwards. However, the hallux is offset from the line of toe number three towards the inside of the trail. It is unlikely that you would confuse a grey heron track with anything else, due to its extreme size. Little egrets are very similar, just smaller. The outer toe, or toe number four, is significantly longer than the inner toe on both species. The claws are relatively insignificant but there is a very large and identifiable metatarsal negative space.

MOORHENS AND COOTS

I have grouped these two together not just because they are found in similar locations but because, in my opinion, they can be very easily confused. Considering what their feet look like, coot tracks should look completely different to those of a moorhen. In reality, however, the lobate fringes around the toes of coots, which should make them unique, often don't show at all. Even when the fleshy lobes do show, they are not always registered as obviously as one would expect. In this case, though, they can still make the toes look significantly fatter than those of the moorhen.

Life-sized right track of a grey heron.

Life-sized left track of a coot.

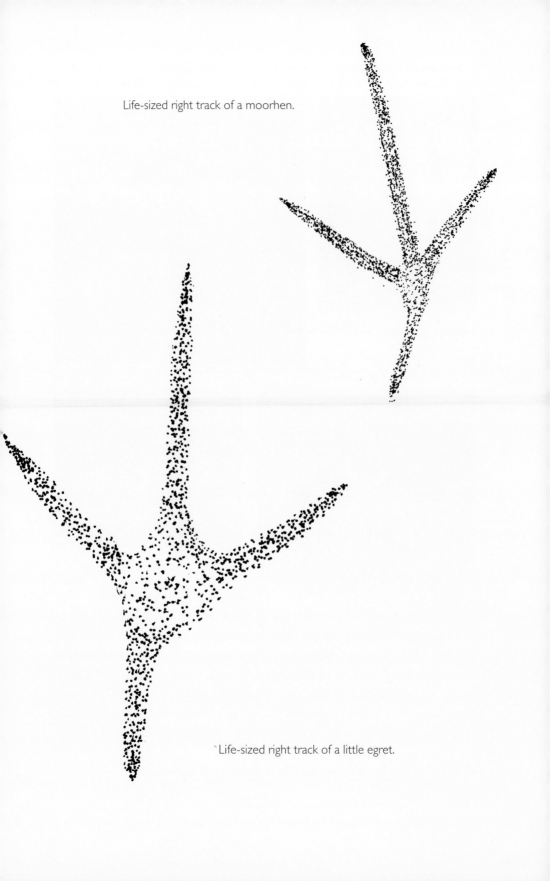

Life-sized right track of a moorhen.

Life-sized right track of a little egret.

Above: Coot left track. (LE)

Right: Moorhen tracks.

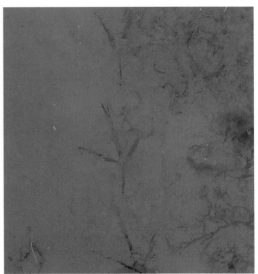

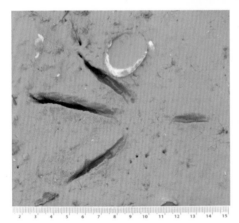

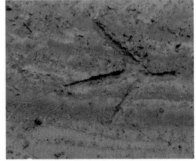

Above: Little egret left track. (LE)

Left: Grey heron track.

Although both birds exhibit the classic bird track, the hallux is relatively short compared to the other toes. The moorhen's toe number three is frequently long relative to its other toes and, together with the hallux, forms a gentle curve through the centre of the track. Coots, on the other hand, have their hallux frequently turned in towards the centre of the trail, to such a degree that it often appears to be in line with toe number four.

Gait: All of the waterbirds described above tend to walk.

Species	L x W (cm) + −
Grey heron (*Ardea cinerea*)	16 x 14
Little egret (*Egretta garzetta*)	13 x 9.0
Coot (*Fulica atra*)	7.0 x 6.2
Moorhen (*Gallinula chloropus*)	9.0 x 6.0

CORVIDS (CROWS)

Most of the corvids (the crow family) are relatively easy to identify due to the very distinctive arrangement and angle of toes. The members of the family described here all exhibit a classic bird track. The main characteristics for the raven, carrion crow, rook and jackdaw are as follows. The inner toe, number two, hugs the leading toe, number three. The hallux is long and tipped with a large curved claw, which shows reliably in the track and often, especially in loose or soft substrate, leaves a drag mark. The other claws are quite robust and frequently show well in the track.

With these four species, the main criteria for identification will be size. Ravens are huge – easily 20 per cent bigger than the next largest corvid.

Life-sized right track of a rook.

Life-sized left track of a carrion crow.

Life-sized right track of a raven.

ROOKS AND CARRION CROWS

These are very similar in size, at least in terms of their tracks. Physically, carrion crows are the stronger, more robust bird, but this doesn't really transfer to the footprint. However, I do believe that rook tracks appear slightly more slender and their toes look shorter and stubbier than those of the carrion crow. This can be very subjective, though, and difficult to prove convincingly to oneself unless you see tracks of the two species together, and even then you may not be 100 per cent sure.

JACKDAWS AND MAGPIES

Jackdaws and magpies are smaller than rooks and carrion crows, but both physically similar to each other in size. They are, however, easier to tell apart than their larger relatives. Look for the hallux of the jackdaw forming a straight line from the metatarsal area. In contrast, the same toe of the magpie curves more in towards the centre of the trail, forming a nice arc through the centre of the track with toe number three. In fact, one could be forgiven for mistaking a magpie track for a small member of the pigeon family. The inner toe sticks out further from the central toe and may therefore also resemble a robust blackbird track.

Life-sized right track of a magpie.

Life-sized right track of a jackdaw.

JAY

The jay is exceptional within the crow family having track features all of its own, although it is still technically a classic bird track. However, with jays, both toes two and four hug the central toe, number three. There is nothing else of this size in the UK you are likely to confuse a jay track with.

Gait: All of the corvids tend to walk.

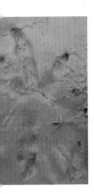

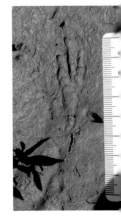

Above left: Raven left track. (LE)

Above centre: Carrion crow right track.

Above right: Rook tracks. (DW)

Below left: Magpie tracks. (DW)

Below centre: Jackdaw tracks. (LE)

Below right: Jay right track.

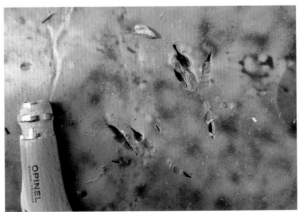

137

Carrion crow trail showing dragging claw.

Species	L x W (cm) + −
Raven (*Corvus corax*)	7.5 x 4.5
Carrion crow (*Corvus coronei*)	6.0 x 3.0
Rook (*Corvus frugilegus*)	6.0 x 2.5
Magpie (*Pica pica*)	4.8 x 2.3
Jackdaw (*Corvus monedula*)	4.8 x 2.5
Jay (*Garrulus glandarius*)	4.6 x 1.6

BIRDS OF PREY AND OWLS

I have only included the buzzard as a representative of birds of prey as it is commonly found hunting for worms on the ground and therefore it will be the most likely tracks to be encountered. I also describe generically the characteristics of owls and believe much more work is needed to be able to separate similar-sized species of owls with confidence.

BUZZARD

The buzzard produces a large track, raven-sized in fact, and this is the species you are most likely to confuse it with. The toe pads are round and obvious, and the hallux is offset slightly from the leading toe (number three) towards the outside of the trial. Toe number two is set closer to 90 degrees from the very large metatarsal area than with any of the corvids. The claws are large and often register strongly in the track ahead of the toes.

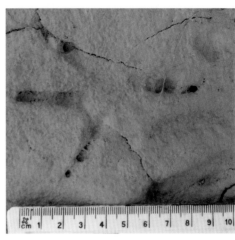

Life-sized right track of buzzard.

Right track of buzzard. (LE)

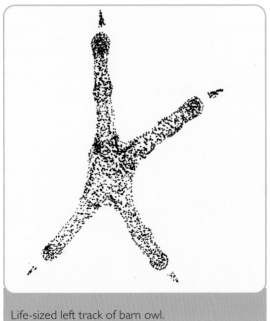

Left track of a tawny owl.

Life-sized left track of barn owl.

Tawny owl tracks.

OWLS

Owls have the ability to direct toes two and three forwards, and toes one and four backwards in the zygodactyl arrangement described above. Unfortunately for the tracker, they can also point toe number two forwards and create a classic bird track arrangement. When in the 'two back and two forward' pattern, the track looks like the letter 'K' or an 'X'.

The only other tracks similar to this that would likely be encountered in the UK are those of the woodpeckers. However, woodpecker tracks are much finer, with less prominent toe pads and claws. Toe pads are also often prominent in owl tracks as are sharp claws. Barn owls and tawny owls are likely to be the most commonly encountered owls and the former seems to have a much longer toe number two than a tawny owl.

Gait: Neither owls nor buzzards spend time walking on the ground, and I have only ever found short trails of either, always paired feet side by side or a couple of walking steps.

Species	Rear L x W (cm) + −
Buzzard (*Buteo buteo*)	7.4 x 4.7
Barn owl (*Tyto alba*)	6.2 x 3.5

Life-sized right track of a woodpigeon.

PIGEONS AND DOVES

Pigeons and doves have very distinctive tracks and have contemporaries across the world with a very similar foot structure, and therefore track impression. Look for a large negative space in the metatarsal area and an arc through the centre of the track caused by the hallux and toe three. There is a general tendency for the feet to point in towards the centre of the trail, hence the expression 'pigeon-toed'.

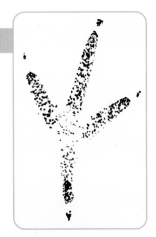

The outer toes are well spaced and angle out away from the track. The claws frequently show. I have illustrated two commonly found species, the largest, our woodpigeon, and the smallest, the collared dove. Both of these can be identified to species level based on morphology and size.

Gait: Pigeons and doves tend to walk.

Above left: Collared dove (above) and woodpigeon (below) tracks. (DW)

Above right: Detail of a woodpigeon track.

Species	L x W (cm) +/ −
Woodpigeon (*Columba palumbus*)	7.5 x 4.5
Collared dove (*Streptopelia decaocto*)	4.6 x 3.0

SMALL BIRDS

I have grouped several commonly found smaller birds into this category as species that are commonly found on the ground and in a wide range of habitats.

Right: Life-sized left track of a blackbird.

Far right: Life-sized right track of a starling.

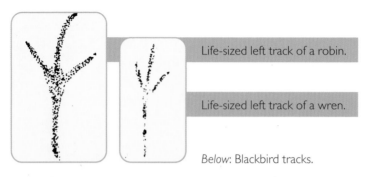

Life-sized left track of a robin.

Life-sized left track of a wren.

Below: Blackbird tracks.

BLACKBIRD AND THRUSHES

Blackbirds and our other thrushes are distinctive in their classic bird track arrangement, and also because of their prominent toe pads, especially at the end of toe three, but also very frequently the hallux. The inner toe often presents at a more acute angle than the outer, and all toes are tipped with fine claws. The negative space can be large, with the metatarsal area sometimes not registering at all.

They tend to skip and hop, so the track pattern can greatly help here. The obvious bulbous toe pad is a feature that is common across the genus *Turdus* and can be found on both the song thrush and mistle thrush in our region, as well as the American robin in North America. The mistle thrush can be confidently identified due to its large size, but more work is needed to separate out other similar-sized thrushes, including our winter migrants from Scandinavia.

Gait: Blackbirds tend to hop and skip.

STARLING

Starling tracks are superficially similar to those of blackbirds – certainly in size – but look out for the distinct lack of bulbous toe pads. The tip of toe three can bend in towards the centre of the trail, and the hallux is also curved towards the centre of the trail, unlike in the blackbird, which is slightly straighter.

Starlings are also quite gregarious birds and so are likely to land on the ground in flocks and leave multiple tracks. Their tracks have smaller negative space in relation to the general size of the track than blackbirds, but with similar fine claws.

Gait: Starlings tend to walk.

Above: Starling left track.

Left: Starling tracks.

Right: Starling tracks showing some claw drag (DW)

Left track of a robin.

ROBIN

Robin tracks are smaller than those of the blackbird and starling, not as much in length and width as you might suspect, but certainly in robustness. The robin is a frequent visitor to the ground and their tracks are distinctive due to the very flexible nature of the tip of toe three. This is frequently curved in quite an extreme way towards the centre of the trail. The two outer toes tend to point out to the sides of the trail at similar angles to each other.

Gait: Robins tend to hop.

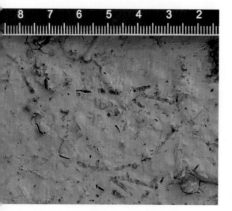

Wren tracks. (DW)

WREN

Wren tracks are fairly obvious, due to their small size and the extreme length of the hallux. The outer toes are angled out from the centre in a similar way to each other, and frequently the metatarsal area doesn't register, leaving a relatively large negative space. The claw on the hallux often registers, making this toe, at first glance, appear even longer than it is.

Gait: Wrens tend to hop.

Species	Rear L x W (cm) +/ −
Blackbird (*Turdus merula*)	4.0 x 2.2
Starling (*Sturnus vulgaris*)	4.0 x 1.8
Robin (*Erithracus rubecula*)	3.7 x 1.6
Wren (*Troglodytes troglodytes*)	2.5 x 0.8

GAME BIRDS

All three of the game birds described below frequently show a downwards curve at the end of the inner toe, number two. When the hallux does show, it angles in towards the trail. Structurally, they are similar to waders. However, none of the game birds have any form of webbing between the toes (like some waders do).

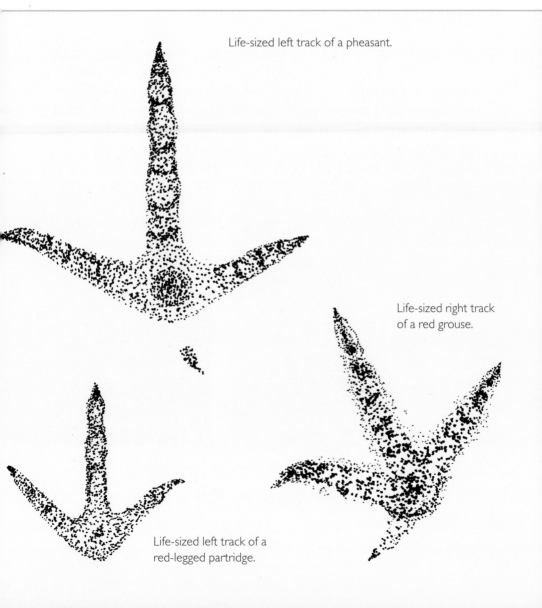

Life-sized left track of a pheasant.

Life-sized right track of a red grouse.

Life-sized left track of a red-legged partridge.

PHEASANT

The pheasant is perhaps the largest game bird track commonly encountered in the UK (unless we include domesticated chickens and turkeys), and size will be the major consideration in identification. Together with the features already described, look out for the metatarsal area which frequently shows as a large dot.

RED GROUSE

The red grouse is also a large bird similar to a pheasant, but with a slightly shorter outer toe four. Its feet are feathered and although this may not show clearly enough to recognise this feature as feathers, it will often distort the track and make it appear either larger than it should be, or fuzzy around the edges. Habitat and region will be a major clue to the identification of this bird's tracks. The metatarsal area registers as a circle.

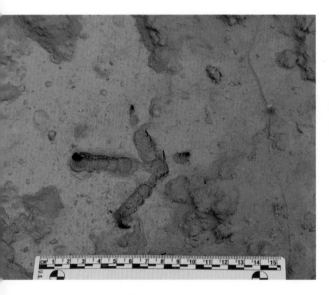 

Above left: Pheasant left track.

Above right: Red grouse right track. (DW)

RED-LEGGED PARTRIDGE

Partridge tracks looks like a small version of pheasant tracks, perhaps half the size but with a less prominent metatarsal 'dot'.

Gait: Game birds tend to walk and run.

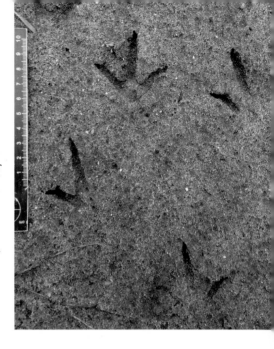

Red-legged partridge tracks. (DW)

Species	Rear L x W (cm) +/ −
Pheasant (*Phasianus colchicus*)	7.0 x 7.5
Red grouse (*Lagopus lagopus scotica*)	6.0 x 6.5
Red-legged partridge (*Alectoris rufa*)	4.5 x 4.5

WADERS

Waders have a foot structure very similar to that of game birds but may also show partial webbing between the outer and central toes. Check also for the presence of the hallux as this can be diagnostic in identification. I describe several species here that are commonly found, together with their general characteristics. They are divided roughly by size.

Life-sized right track of curlew.

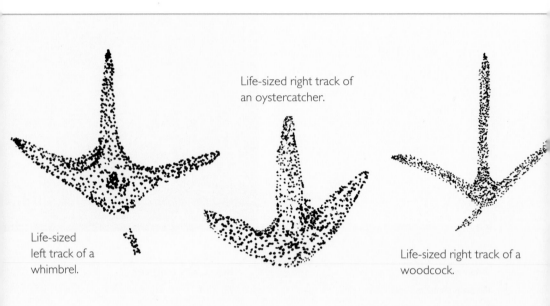

Life-sized right track of
an oystercatcher.

Life-sized
left track of a
whimbrel.

Life-sized right track of a
woodcock.

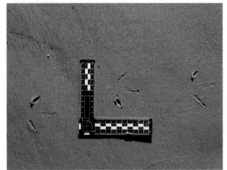

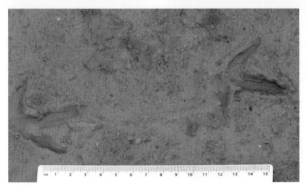

Above left: Curlew trail.

Above centre: Curlew trail.
(DW)

Above right: Whimbrel
tracks.

Right: Oystercatcher tracks.

Far right: Oystercatcher
tracks. (DW)

LARGE WADERS

CURLEW

The curlew is likely to be one of the largest waders encountered and is identifiable with the angle the outer toes are set to the central toe; it comes closer to 90 degrees than most other birds. There is webbing between toes two and three, and between three and four. The metatarsus registers weakly, and the hallux is frequently absent in the track. Whimbrel tracks are very similar to those of the curlew, only smaller.

OYSTERCATCHER

Oystercatchers have webbing between toes three and four, and toe four is angled up more than most waders, giving a lopsided look to the track. The hallux doesn't show at all and the toes can vary in different substrates from quite thin and linear, to quite robust and tapering like a leaf blade.

WOODCOCK

Woodcock tracks can look a little like slender, skinny pheasant tracks. They have no webbing showing in the track and a fairly small metatarsal area that forms a neat dot when it registers in good substrate. The hallux registers frequently and, like many waders, this is in line with toe four.

Woodcock tracks. (LE)

Snipe trail with probe holes. (LE)

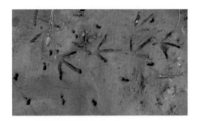

SNIPE

Snipe tracks are very similar to woodcock. They are a little smaller but with very much the same foot structure and therefore easily confusable. Location and habitat are a good aid to separating the two species.

SMALL WADERS

LAPWING

The lapwing has partial webbing between toes three and four but with no hallux showing in the track.

TURNSTONE

No webbing shows in the track, but both the hallux and the metatarsal area register well.

SANDERLING

This is the smallest wader described here. There is weak registration of the metatarsal area, and no hallux shows in the tracks.

Gait: Waders walk and run.

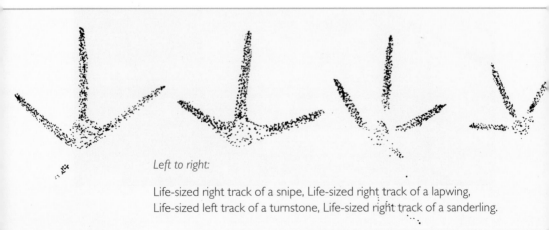

Left to right:

Life-sized right track of a snipe, Life-sized right track of a lapwing, Life-sized left track of a turnstone, Life-sized right track of a sanderling.

Species	L x W (cm) +/ −
Curlew (*Numenius arqata*)	4.8 x 6.2
Whimbrel (*Numenius phaeopus*)	4.0 x 5.0
Oystercatcher (*Haematopus ostralegus*)	4.0 x 4.0
Woodcock (*Scolopax rusticola*)	4.0 x 4.5
Snipe (*Gallinago gallinago*)	3.4 x 4.0
Lapwing (*Vanellus vanellus*)	2.8 x 3.4
Turnstone (*Arenaria interpres*)	2.6 x 3.0
Sanderling (*Calidris alba*)	1.7 x 2.2

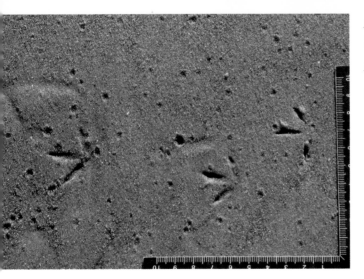

Above right: Turnstone trail. (DW)

Above Left: Lapwing tracks. (LE)

Left: Sanderling tracks. (DW)

WEBBED BIRDS

A tracker may be forgiven for thinking that web-footed birds would be easy to characterise, purely because of their web. However, in very many substrates the web unfortunately doesn't register in the track and this can make identification difficult. Look at the outer toes, which often exhibit a curve along their outer edge. I like to imagine the membrane of the webbing pulling the toes into an arc.

This group of web-footed birds can be broken down into three main types, at least for the purposes of this book. Ducks and geese, gulls and terns, and cormorants. These groupings are based on the leading edge of the webbing, which forms a different shape in each set (due to differences in relative toe lengths). Cormorants are totipalmate, which requires its own distinction.

MUTE SWAN

These are the largest webbed tracks encountered in our region. The hallux doesn't show, and the metatarsal area is a perfect circle that frequently registers.

DUCKS AND GEESE

There is a crossover size-wise between large ducks and small geese. I have illustrated the Canada goose and the mallard and shelduck. Ducks of this type (the dabbling ducks) have an extra flap of webbing on the outside of toe number two. In the track, this can be seen either in detail or as what looks like a very fat toe depending on the quality of the substrate. This feature seems to be missing in geese, or at least in the geese I have studied.

The dabbling ducks also regularly show the hallux, which is not the case in the geese (at least not in Canada geese). Although toe number two is shorter, both it and toe four extend high in the track on geese and ducks. They finish just below leading toe three and so the 'curtain' edge of the webbing is fairly straight.

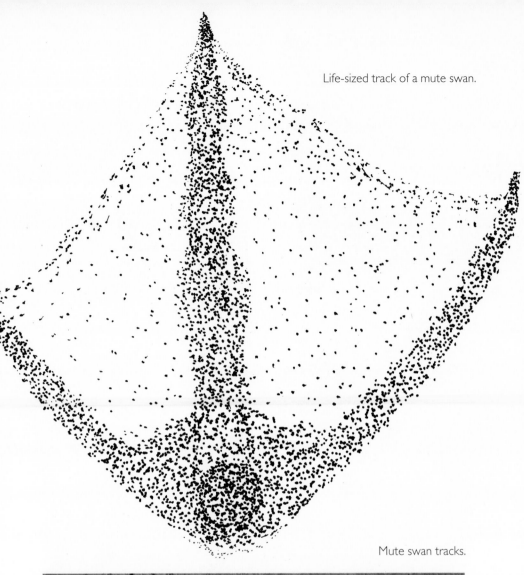

Life-sized track of a mute swan.

Mute swan tracks.

153

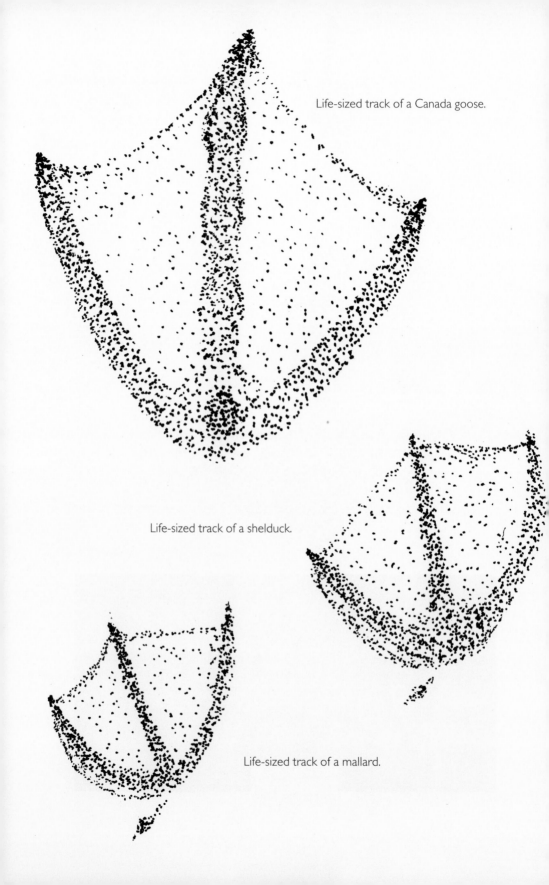

Life-sized track of a Canada goose.

Life-sized track of a shelduck.

Life-sized track of a mallard.

Gait: Ducks and geese tend to walk and dabbling ducks, especially, turn their feet into the trail and walk pigeon-toed. The expression 'duck-footed', in humans, annoyingly refers to feet that turn out and is no help here at all.

The exceptions to the general goose/duck structure of bent outer toes and extra membranes are the diving ducks and other fish eaters, such as the mergansers. They have a much straighter outer edge to toes two and four, and the track is generally narrower in relation to its width when compared with both dabbling ducks and geese. This is yet another area in need of further work in the realm of bird tracks. The track illustrated below is a diving duck and I believe it to be a pochard, but I am not 100 per cent certain.

 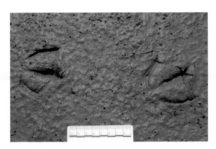 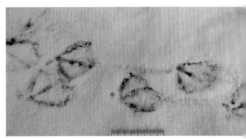

Above left: Canada goose track. (DW)

Above centre: Shelduck track. Note the broad impression on the inner toe.

Above right: Mallard trail in the snow. (LE)

Unknown diving duck.

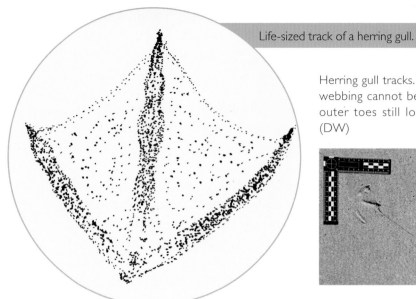

Life-sized track of a herring gull.

Herring gull tracks. Note that the webbing cannot be seen but the outer toes still look 'pulled in'. (DW)

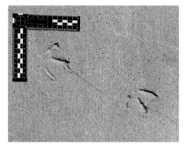

GULLS

Life-sized track of black-headed gull.

These are, at first glance, very similar to duck and geese tracks. They range in size from the relatively small black-headed gull to the herring gull and the enormous great black-backed gull. Generally, as a group, they are less likely to register the hallux than ducks and geese. The outer toes do not seem to extend as far into the track as the previous group and this creates a scooped shape in the leading edge of the webbing, which I find quite reliable. Even when the webbing isn't obvious, hopefully the toe length is.

Black-headed gull trail. (DW)

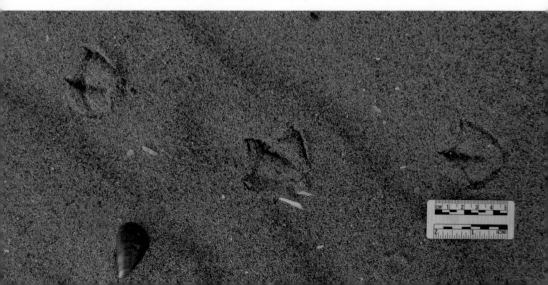

Life-sized track of an Arctic tern.

TERNS

These are the smallest web-footed birds described here. They have even shorter outer toes than the gulls and have an extreme scoop in the leading edge of the webbing. The hallux also registers in the track more reliably in this group of birds.

Gait: Gulls and terns walk and run.

Arctic tern trail. (DW)

CORMORANT

Cormorants are unique and distinctive when the full track registers. The webbing between all the toes, including between the hallux and toe one, should make it obvious. Unfortunately, it isn't always obvious as the webbing doesn't always show. However, due to the arrangement of the webbing and the way the foot orientates, look for toe number four appearing to be the longest and the other toes reducing in size towards the inside of the trail.

Gait: Cormorants tend not to move around very much, and when I have seen them it has always been a walk. They will run, however, to get up speed for take-off.

Left: Cormorant tracks. (DW)

Life-sized track of a comorant.

Species	L x W (cm) +/ −
Mute swan (*Cygnus olor*)	16.5 x 14
Canada goose (*Branta canadensis*)	11 x 10.5
Cormorant (*Phalacrocorax carbo*)	10.5 8.5
Herring gull (*Larus argentatus*)	6.3 x 6.8
Shelduck (*Tadorna tadorna*)	6.0 x 6.0
Mallard (*Anas platyrhynchos*)	4.5 x 5.0
Black-headed gull (*Chroicocephalus ridibundis*)	4.5 x 4.2
Arctic tern (*Sterna paradisaeai*)	2.5 x 2.5

Having read these descriptions, I hope you can appreciate the degree of uncertainty that currently exists in identifying certain bird groups to species level. Fellow trackers and I are constantly exploring this area. We will, I am sure, find many more birds that can be positively identified from their tracks. Equally, we may find that, for example, separating the various small gull species is not possible. Either way, at least a question will have been answered.

BIRD GAITS AND TRACK PATTERNS

Birds gaits are less complicated than mammals in that there are only two feet to worry about, which does limit confusion. Birds will walk, run, hop or skip and these gaits are fairly easy to identify using some of the basic principles already outlined for mammals.

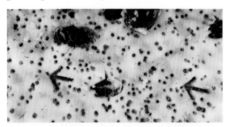

Top: Pheasant running. Note the long stride and narrow straddle. A size 8 (EU 42) boot is at the top of the photo for scale.

Bottom: By comparison, this is the shorter stride of a walking bird.

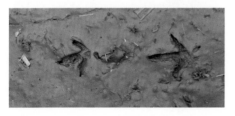

Blackbird in a skipping gait.

Side-by-side house sparrow tracks, indicative of these birds' normal hopping gait.

Walks, for example, show a short stride and a wide straddle. When the same bird runs, the straddle narrows, and the stride lengthens. However, straddle may not be as obvious a way to separate gaits as it is in mammals.

Hops are employed by birds which are not necessarily at their most comfortable on the ground and these show as paired, parallel tracks. Skips also involve the feet being paired but, unlike hops, the feet hit the ground at slightly different times and leave trails with one of the pair in front of the other.

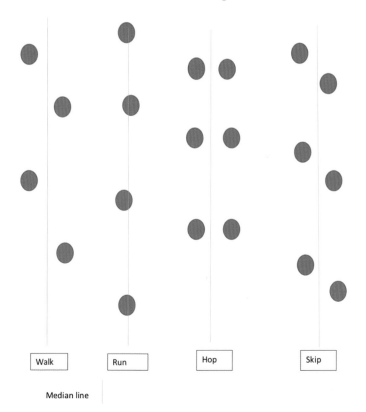

Walk   Run   Hop   Skip

Median line

REPTILE AND AMPHIBIAN TRACKS

The UK is home to six native species of reptile: three snakes and three lizards. Representing the snakes are grass snake, smooth snake and adder, with the slow worm and sand and common lizards representing the lizards. There are a few colonies of exotic reptiles, including the green and wall lizards, the Aesculapian snake and the red-eared terrapin, or slider. The European pond terrapin is also present. It was native several thousand years ago and there is some speculation that it's still present today, perhaps a remnant of that population, although that seems a little unlikely.

In terms of amphibians, we have as our native animals three species of newts: palmate, smooth and great-crested; two toads – the natterjack and the common toad; and two frogs – the common frog and the reintroduced pool frog. There are several amphibian escapees that are known to be breeding or at least surviving long-term in the UK. If added together with our native animals, then our reptile and amphibian species list rises to eighteen at the time of writing.

Within the scope of this guide, I focus on identifying the broad groups of frogs, toads, newts, lizards, snakes and terrapins. It could be that it will be possible to identify these little folks to species level but for now recognising the broad groups at all is our aim.

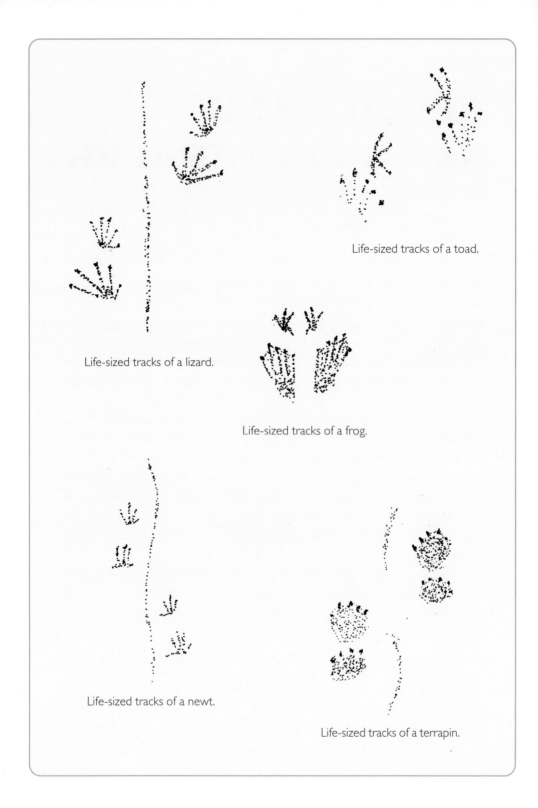

Life-sized tracks of a toad.

Life-sized tracks of a lizard.

Life-sized tracks of a frog.

Life-sized tracks of a newt.

Life-sized tracks of a terrapin.

FROGS AND TOADS

Both of these groups have four toes on the front feet and five on the back. They can be difficult to separate, but as a rule, frogs tend to hop and toads tend to walk. However, both species can do either but generally don't drop out of their baseline gait for extended periods of time. Long walking trails, for example, are most likely to be toads.

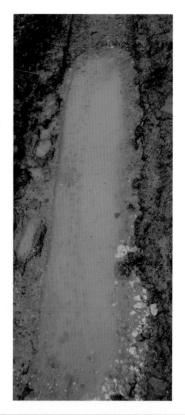

Right: Toad trail registering in the mud of a shallow puddle.

Below: Details of an underwater toad trail.

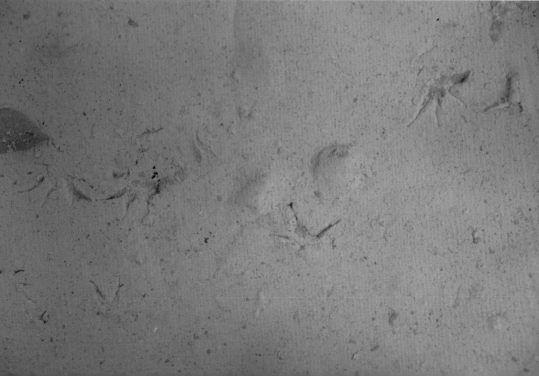

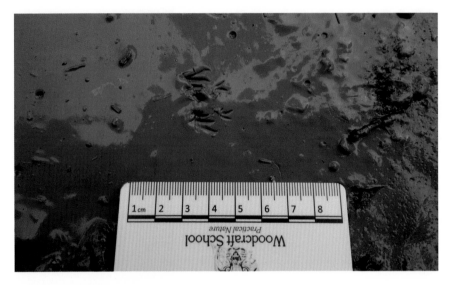

Frogs have a similar track structure to toads, but their different modes of locomotion are a big help in identification.

Both frogs and toads leave a distinct pattern, with the front tracks consisting of four fingers pointing into the trail at or close to 90 degrees from the direction of travel. The rear tracks often present as a line of dots caused by toes/claws one to four in a line radiating out from the centre of the trail. Toe five can often be seen just below toe four.

Sometimes belly marks may be seen, as may the webbing of the rear feet in good substrates. Front tracks of toads may be obliterated by the rears.

NEWTS

Newts have four toes on the front foot and five on the back foot, and the feet register close together. They also leave a distinct tail track in substrate that will register such fine detail. Without the definition found in a good tracking medium that may show the number of toes, newt trails can be confused with lizards. However, to my mind, they always seem to be swimming through the landscape and their trails are therefore very sinuous.

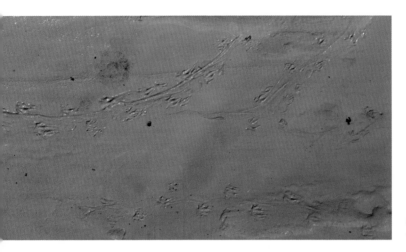

Left: Newt tracks.

LIZARDS

Lizards have five toes on both the front and rear, and also have claws. However, in practice, in my experience at least, it is very rare to find much detail in the tracks themselves. I find detailed lizard trails much less frequently than newts, mostly due to habitat and therefore the substrates involved. Look for a less sinuous trail to help with confirmation. The trail is often shown as a straight-line tail drag, as can be seen in the images below.

Above: Lizard trail.

SNAKES AND SLOW WORMS

These creatures are very similar physically and so have similar, if not identical, methods of using their bodies to move. I have found lots of 'snake-like' trails, but have to say, I am unable to identify them to species level without some other clues. For example, a female grass snake can reach a far greater size than any of our other snakes, but that does not mean I can tell a small grass snake from a smooth snake, for example.

Trails can be fairly straight, or wonderfully arched and sweeping, or a little of both. This is dependent on the resistance they encounter, and this determines the way they move. As a rule of thumb, resistance means an arching trail, as would happen if the animal travelled uphill. Straighter trails are more likely to be found going downhill or on level ground.

Snake trail.

166

TERRAPINS

After the popularity of a certain Hollywood movie franchise, many terrapins were bought as pets. Sadly, as is often the case, after the enthusiasm for the sword-wielding reptiles subsided, they become unwanted pets. Many have been released and are thriving, or at least semi-thriving, in parts of our landscape. It has previously been thought that the sustained long periods of hot weather needed for these animals to breed do not occur in the UK. However, there has been a sighting of a very young animal in London, which may suggest that, at least in some exceptional years, breeding may be possible. With the climate-warming we are

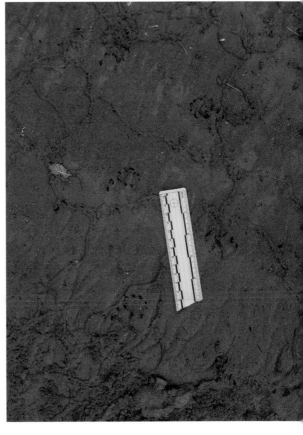

Typical terrapin/turtle trail. (KC)

undergoing at the moment, these voracious predators of fish and young waterbirds may be a real problem in years to come. They are therefore something that wildlife trackers should be alert to, especially as we are often surveying around bodies of water.

Terrapins have five toes on the front and rear feet, and often walk in an understepped fashion, creating tramlines of tracks either side of the centre of the trail, which may also show tail drag. Drag from the underside of the shell may also show in the track.

INVERTEBRATE TRACKS

If a person stares intently at the ground for long enough, at some point they will notice the telltale trails of our smallest creatures. Time and space restrictions mean I can only pay lip service to this group of animals, and I am sure there is a much bigger story to be told here. I include some principles only, so the tracker can at least get a general idea of who made the tracks they may be finding.

Left to right:

Beetle trail drawing, Spider trail drawing, Worm trail drawing, Millipede trail drawing, Caterpillar trail drawing.

Below: Beetle trail in sand.

Beetle trail in water.

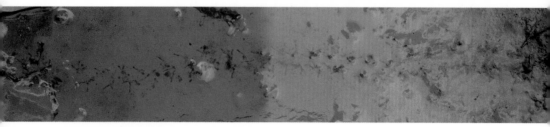

BEETLES

Beetle trails are a regular feature in drying puddles and sand. Several species regularly leave trails and with further study it will, I believe, be possible to identify many of them to species level. Several species leave body drags, while others stand on tall legs with their bodies clear of the ground. Look out for the three marks on each side of the trail that represent the six legs of this group of insects. The front two legs and rear two legs leave tracks pointing in the direction of travel, while the middle legs leave tracks pointing away from the trail.

SPIDERS

Spiders leave similar trails to beetles but have eight legs, and so show four marks on either side of the trail. It does take good substrate for all eight legs to show, but when they do, they can resemble tiny bird tracks.

CATERPILLARS

Often found on the ground, the most common version of these trails looks like opposite pairs of dots forming a tramline. The dots are caused by feet-like structures that are attached to the segmented sections of the larval body.

Above: Trail of an exhausted bee.

Above left: Crab tracks.

Above right: Worm trail.

Right: Woodlouse tracks.

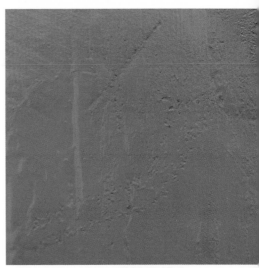

Below: This is a large African species of millipede, but the track pattern is the same as for our smaller European species.

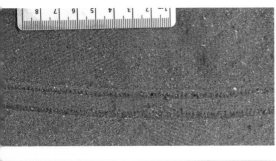

Above: The trail of a slug is continuous.

Right: The trail of a snail shows intermittent deposits of slime.

MILLIPEDES

Millipedes leave similar trails to caterpillars, but the dots are caused by true moving legs and are much finer. They are much more tightly packed together and, in some substrates, it can be difficult to see the individual dots, which rather appear as a continuous line. They do not generally make a trough with their bodies.

WORMS

Worms trails of various size and shape are frequently encountered in soft mud, particularly on the edge of drying puddles. Often the individual segments of the worms' body can be seen. They are frequently very sinuous trails and leave a little trough made by the body.

SLUGS AND SNAILS

These molluscs are identified by their slime trail, which on a slug is continuous and, on a snail, tends to stop and start.

CRABS

Including the claws, crabs have ten legs – and they use them to great effect in moving sideways along a trail. The most commonly encountered crab tracks are in sand and consists of numerous marks made by the claws at the end of their legs. Once seen they are unmistakable.

PART 2

SIGN

SCAT

Scatology is not necessarily the most attractive subject to talk about, but scat is, along with footprints, the most commonly encountered type of sign to be found in the landscape.

Location can be important when trying to establish the owner of any scat you find. Many species use scat to advertise their presence and may, therefore, deposit it on raised areas or in the middle of trails. Some may leave it in dug latrines, while others may deposit lots of scat in the same area, creating a latrine or midden, thereby attracting attention to the scat producer. Some scat may be deposited differently depending on the time of year and therefore the behaviour pattern of that particular creature.

Location can be key to identification. This badger scat is placed in a dug latrine.

Morphology, as with many things in nature, is very important. We can divide scat into a few main categories which can then be further subdivided into types. The categories I tend to use are: pelleted, sausages, tapering twists, and clumps and splats – any one of which, I hope you will agree, would be a delight to come across. The final category is a bit more of a mouthful (perish the thought!) – things that look like mammal scat but aren't.

This cherry-filled red fox scat can be difficult to identify due to its consistency.

The content of scat can be hugely variable depending on the time of year and the food sources available. In winter, a fox scat may be in the form of a classic carnivore twist and be full of hair and bits of feather and bone. The same animal may, in the spring and summer, produce a less obvious-shaped scat full of beetle wing cases or mud from the worms it consumes. In the autumn, it may also gorge on fruit (such as cherries) and produce shapeless splats. Be aware that hair in small quantities may come from the animal grooming itself and not necessarily indicate a carnivore's consumed prey.

Smell is the final key aid in identifying scat. Our blackberry-filled fox splat mentioned above may look exactly like the blackberry-filled splat of a badger. Sometimes the difference is only revealed by the slightly musky badger odour verses the clinging 'back-of-the-throat' stench of the fox.

Caution should be exhibited when smelling scats, though, as they can cause disease. With some droppings, especially when fresh, it is not necessary to stick your nose particularly close to know exactly who did it. Do take precautions when examining scat, though. Breaking it open to reveal its contents can be done with a stick at arm's length, so there is no real reason to pick it up. It is possible to inhale all kinds of nasties from scat, so please do be careful.

PELLETED

I use the word 'pelleted' to distinguish this group from bird pellets. This is scat that is round or partially cylindrical, although the length to width ratio is never so great as to be sausage-like. Pelleted scat is all going to belong to three main groups of animals: lagomorphs, squirrels and ungulates.

Size can be important when separating species with similar-shaped scat. For those that produce a quantity of pellets, take the average size within the group of pellets in front of you. Any animal can produce the odd large and small scat, so finding the middle ground can be important. In my experience, piles of scat are likely to contain only the occasional over- or undersized scat.

LAGOMORPHS

In our region, lagomorphs are represented by one species of rabbit and two species of hare. Collectively, they serve to illustrate the potential for similar animals to deposit very similar looking scat in different ways. They also show that the same species of an animal may deposit scat differently, depending on sex and territoriality.

Lagomorphs perform coprophagy which, in other words, means they eat their own excrement. I will let that sink in for a moment before mentioning that they often eat their droppings directly from their own anus. The reason for this is to extract maximum enrichment from the hard-to-digest cellulose in their herbivorous diet. In addition to this double digestion strategy, they also have a greatly enlarged caecum, which is a pouch connected to the large intestine that contains cellulose-digesting bacteria. Many herbivorous animals have an enlarged caecum, as do some birds.

What is left in the scat of lagomorphs after their double dose of nutrient extraction is very fibrous and coarse. The outer surface of the scat is frequently straw-coloured, with the fibres of plant material visible. This can be quite useful to avoid confusion with deer scat, which tends to be less fibrous and straw-like, although I have found red deer scat on poor ground that is fibrous.

Above left: Rabbit scat on a scent mound.

Above right: Hare scat.

RABBIT SCAT

Often rabbit scat is round, or only slightly flattened into a chunky disc. Latrines are often
created on high points, very typically ant hills
and mole hills, for scent-marking purposes.
Scat can also be found in scrapes, especially

Rabbit scats.

at the edges of paths used by rabbits. This scat may also be slightly pinched
into a small nipple at one end, making it confusable with smaller deer
species, although it is never as cylinder-like as deer scat. Rabbit scat may also
be dropped randomly as the animals move around in their territory. In terms
of size, the pellets are unlikely to be much bigger than a large garden pea.

HARES

Hares do not advertise themselves or defend territories in the same way
as rabbits, so their droppings will not be found in any quantity nor associated with mounds or scrapes. They are very similar in appearance and
texture to rabbit scat and may be slightly flattened in the same way. They
are, however, generally much bigger, and instead of garden pea size are
much more on the scale of a large blueberry.

So, it is good practice to scout around the local area where you find
any lagomorph scat to try to find any other associated sign that will help
to determine which species it belongs to.

SQUIRRELS

Squirrel scat (and this applies to both grey and red squirrels) is seldom found, as they drop it randomly as they go about their business. You may, however, find it associated with feeding sign and anywhere they regularly cross the landscape, such as on leaning trees or the tops of fences. What makes squirrel scat so distinctive is its variability. It can look like a deformed and squashed rabbit scat but can also appear similar to rat scat (see below), so it can be either pellet or sausage shaped. If you find scat that doesn't quite look like rabbit and doesn't quite look like rat, especially in a likely location, then start to consider squirrel. Squirrel scat does not smell strongly, which may also help separate it from other rodent species.

DEER

Deer have very distinctive scat in the form of cylindrical pellets that are longer than they are wide, and frequently with a pinched nipple at one end. When the animals have plenty of moisture in the diet, the individual pellets, or fewmets, may lump together to form a 'crottie'. Within this mass, the individual pellets can often still be seen. However, in certain situations, deer scat may come out as a formless splat.

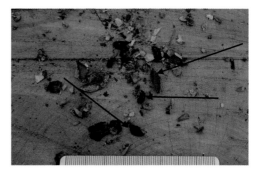

Above: Greysquirrel scat found on a feeding table.

Below: The green colour and sheen of the membrane denotes a fresh deer scat.

Scats of different ages denote a latrine-using species, in this case Chinese water deer.

When deer scat first leaves the body there is a membrane around each individual pellet – they may be green, and/or joined together into a long sausage. When trailing, noticing the presence of a membrane, colour and form of deer scat may help indicate the age of the scat and, therefore, how close you might be to the deer.

There is significant overlap in the size of pellets from the various deer species. I tend to use my little fingernail as a gauge to judge size. If a scat fits on the nail and I can see most of my nail around it, it's muntjac size. If it covers my nail completely or almost completely, it's roe size, and if it overhangs the nail significantly it's fallow. Try using a simple guide like this for the deer in your region – and don't lick your fingers afterwards … Keep in mind that there will be some size differences in deer scat associated with whether the animal is male or female, young or adult.

There are also domesticated animals to be included in this pelleted category, particularly goats, sheep and increasingly exotic animals such as alpacas and llamas.

WILD BOAR AND PIGS

Like deer, wild boar can also produce varied scat that may, at certain times of year and under certain dry diets, be in the form of individual pellets or lumped together. Both wild boar and deer scat has a very distinctive and, I would say, unpleasant smell.

Left: Wild boar scat.

Right: Fallow deer 'crotties'.

Top left: There is always a possibility of anomalies, these roe deer scats include one or two extra long pellets.

Top right: Reeves' muntjac deer scat.

Left: Red deer scat

INSECTS

You may occasionally come across the scat of large hawk moth caterpillars which can be very pellet-like, although often with little striations running along the length of the scat. They can be surprisingly large, so much so that 'insect' may not immediately be your first thought.

Hawk moth caterpillar scat.

TOADS

Toads will also produce small pellets if they have been feeding predominantly on insects with a strong exoskeleton as opposed to soft-bodied creatures like snails and worms. They are usually extremely friable, and often fall apart with handling.

Toad scat. This is from an American species but is identical to the type of scat produced by European toads. (DM)

181

SAUSAGES

. . . .

Sausage scat is longer than it is wide, but doesn't usually taper or twist. It is produced by some fairly big mammals, and also our smallest.

RODENTS

I refer here specifically to mice, rats and voles, all of which produce droppings in great quantities. Location can be key to identification as mice and rats tend to scat on the move, with random scat found on their travel routes or, in fact, pretty much anywhere that they have visited. Their scat tends towards being pointed at both ends, and often has an irregular, almost crusty surface, presumably as a result of their diverse opportunist diet. Scat of varying ages may be found along likely travel routes and in feeding areas. As you can probably tell from my own knowledge of such things, I don't waste my weekends!

Voles tend to deposit scat in latrines and therefore it may be found in piles. Field voles, for example, will leave scat at junctions along their runs which are quite easy to find in long grass areas. Water voles, which are significantly larger than field voles, leave scat in piles, often on a little flat area or shelf close to the water. They paddle down the pile of scat with their

Left and middle: Water vole latrine.

Right: Note the blunted ends of this bank vole scat.

feet, presumably helping to distribute their odour as they travel. 'Ratty' from Kenneth Grahame's *The Wind in the Willows* was, in fact, a water vole and therefore engaged in this habit. In contrast to mice and rat scat, vole scat is much more rounded at each end and has a smooth surface texture. Field vole scat tends to be greener (as a result of its specialist herbaceous plant diet) in comparison to the darker colour of bank voles.

Top row: Brown rat and black rat.
Bottom row: Water vole and rabbit.

Size and shape are key to separating mice from rats, and the smaller voles from water voles. Rat scat is fairly pungent, but the two species, the extremely rare black rat and the brown rat, have very similar scat.

I have not yet found a way to reliably separate wood mouse, yellow-necked mouse and house mouse scat. The scat of other rodents, such as the hazel dormouse and harvest mouse, is seldom, if ever, encountered.

INSECTIVORES

The sausage-shaped scat of insectivores all tends to resemble bat droppings, the smaller ones looking superficially like mouse scat. Close inspection should reveal an extremely crusty surface and the remains of insect parts.

Hedgehog scat is perhaps the most often encountered of this group, being found on garden lawns and dropped randomly during nightly hunting expeditions. These droppings look huge in comparison to the animal and hedgehog may not be your first thought when thinking of the culprit. Once identification is established, your second thought may be one of sympathy.

Above left: Hedgehog scat above, bat scat below.

Above right: Shrew scat.

Mole scat.

I have only once found shrew scat, with this being in association with some tracks that I discovered first. As with all animals, insectivore scat may vary considerably with diet. There is little or no smell to the scat of insectivores.

BADGERS

Although they are technically carnivores, badger scat lacks the classic carnivore tapering twist. Badgers have an omnivorous diet and given a choice, they will eat a great deal of insect protein, especially worms. Consequently, their scat can appear very muddy from the high soil content. Badgers very often use dug latrines, but they will relieve themselves in the middle of their trails as well. I find this especially in late summer when there is an abundance of fruit – I guess there is nothing like a high fruit diet to 'keep you regular' and it could be these guys just get caught short and can't make it to their latrine. I am sure we have all been there!

I used to say to my students that what I like to think of as 'urgent scatting' happens occasionally, but I have now found so much of this that I now say it frequently happens. In this fruit diet situation, it often resembles splats, but classically the wormy, muddy badger scat looks as if it has been pushed through a giant cake icing bag.

In dry weather, badgers may not be able to get a decent insect meal, especially if the worms leave the soil surface. In these conditions, badgers will push cereal crops down to eat the seeds, or they will raid pheasant feeders. Scat from this sort of diet will then start to resemble granola bars. Unlike foxes, I have also found the small bones of mammals in badger scat, but they do come out in fragile state and can be crushed to powder, presumably weakened by the digestive juices of the animal's gut.

Badger 'granola'(!) scat.

Badger scat often smells quite earthy, but with a musky odour from the anal glands that all the mustelids have. Occasionally this anal secretion is found in and on the scat.

CATS

Cats in our region refer to the Eurasian lynx (hopefully, if reintroduced), wildcat and domestic cats. Cat scat is often fairly even in width along its length, although it can be tapered at the very end. It is a very abrupt taper, though, and not the gradual reduction in width found with other carnivore scat. This is due to the mechanics of how they feed, generally licking the meat from the bones of their prey, and therefore not needing to protect the gut wall from damage caused by bone shards (see below). This also means that there is little hair and bone visible in their scat. Any hair that is present often belongs to the animal itself.

Domestic cats fed on proprietary foods, as is the case with dogs, tend to create moist, soft scat. It tends to be segmented, often breaking up into smaller parts. Sometimes it is found buried, or partially buried, but may be out in the open on a platform, in the middle of trail or at a trail junction as an advertisement. Cat scat smells strongly and is, in wild felids, very firm and hard when pressed with a stick.

BATS

Bat scat is often easier to find than their terrestrial counterparts. Generically, bat scat is crusty, often shiny with insect remains, and crumbles easily between the fingers. Mice and rat scat, which can be confused with bat, will smear between the fingers. Do wash your hands after squashing scat in this way.

It is possible to identify a very few bats' scat to species by shape, size and location. However, many species' scat is so similar looking that it may only be possible to roughly group them. Look for scat on window sills and around old trees, especially caught up in cobwebs, as well as in roof spaces and church belfries, etc. I have included information below from friend, CyberTracker enthusiast and bat specialist, Richard Law.

Small bats: pipistrelles, whiskered, Brandt's and alcathoe.

Medium bats: long-eared and the other *Myotis* species, natterer's, Daubenton's, Bechstein's, etc.

Large bats: noctule, serotine, Leisler's and mouse-eared.

Although it is difficult to identify many bats to species level, long-eared bat scat is always twisty. However, with age, even these tend to break up and can appear as smaller droppings. Also, they tend to dry out very rapidly, as mostly they are found in dry environments such as roof voids, so they can shrink and crumble.

SLUGS

Slugs can leave small, soft-looking scat in a sausage shape, often in little lines broken up with gaps between segments of scat. Look for associated feeding signs close by, and also their trails. Slug scat will vary in colour depending on their diet at the time.

Both snail and slug scat is frequently encountered.

TAPERING TWISTS

This scat is formed in sausages, but they taper, tend not to break into small chunks and are generally twisted. In our region, they are exclusively deposited by carnivores.

DOGS

Dog scat also varies considerably with diet. It is possible for domestic dogs to produce scat that looks like any wild canine. Their scat can also look like the sausages described in the previous category. The reality is that most domestic dogs are fed proprietary food, and therefore their scat tends to be less twisty and without the bone fragments and hair that wolf scat, for example, would have. It is often more akin to cat scat although less likely to break into chunks. Should you wish to spend your time breaking scat up with a stick, I am sure you will discover this. Dog scat has a distinctive smell, which I am sure everyone is familiar with, and is often randomly deposited, in the open and sometimes in association with ground scraping.

Above left: European wolf scat.

Above right: Domestic dog scat.

RED FOX

Fox scat is very variable depending on the time of year and, therefore, the diet. They may be full of fruit or equally full of rabbit fur. The classic fox scat will be deposited on a raised point beside or in the centre of a trail and be both tapered and twisted. The contents can include, in addition to the two mentioned above, claws, bone, feather ends, beetle wing cases and grain. I once found the entire skin and claws from a pigeon foot in a fox scat. Look for scat of a variety of ages along trails, as foxes will travel the same routes regularly and scent mark as they go. They may, on occasion, form loose scat that could be confused with a badger's in this state. Small, delicate rodent bones tend not to survive in the scat of foxes.

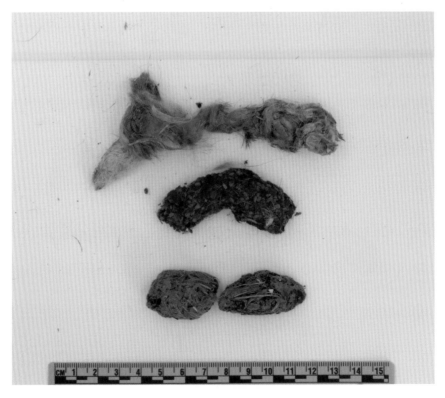

Red fox scats showing a variety of diets in different seasons. Top to bottom, scat containing rabbit fur, seeds and beetles.

Fox scent is very strong and distinctive, and their scat is no exception to this. Unlike the badger, a strong-smelling fox scat will grab you at the back of the throat and stay there. I like to think of it as the scat that just keeps on giving. I have mentioned this before, but be very careful with smelling scat, especially from carnivores.

Left: Red fox scat deposited on a high point, in this case, a mole hill.

Below: Large carnivore scat (from the top): Iberian wolf, Eurasian lynx, Scottish wildcat and badger on a slightly firmer diet than its usual worms.

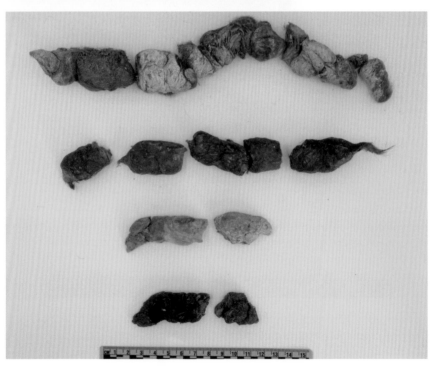

AMERICAN MINK

I have found mink scat in a variety of locations, sometimes just deposited across a wide area and presumably randomly, sometimes with apparent purpose. It can often be found near water, as this is a preferred habitat of these creatures, but don't be too fixated on this as they will hunt far from water. The literature suggests – and we have found – that mink will most often travel for new territory or to find a mate along rivers. But males especially, once installed in a territory, will hunt in the surrounding land for rabbits and other prey.

I suspect that with the return of our rather splendid and out-competing otter, mink may turn up in all kinds of other locations. Tracking in North America, the native home for these creatures, I have found mink scat on top of platforms, placed prominently for scent marking. Most of the scat I have found has been black and tarry, and unpleasant smelling. Like many mustelids, they often latrine, and scat may be found in large amounts.

This American mink latrine was found under an upturned boat.

PINE MARTEN

Pine marten scat is perhaps most likely to be confused with foxes, and their scat can be equally varied. This variation includes its shape, to the extent that it may not even show the general carnivore twist. The scat frequently contains fruits, and may be deposited in a territorially prominent place, or not. Reputedly, it smells quite pleasant, although this is not a description I would necessarily use.

POLECAT

This too can resemble smaller fox scat and is of a similar size to pine marten. I have also found it only on very odd occasions. The scat I have found was close to old rabbit burrows and very close to an area where I had found lots of tracks. They are known to make latrines near to their resting areas and are also known to take over rabbit burrows, and so scat can be expected in these places. I also once found what I am sure was a polecat scat under a hedgerow. Polecat scat does smell very strongly, although not, I feel, quite as overpowering as fox. In our region, these creatures feed almost exclusively on rabbits and, to a lesser extent, small rodents, so it would be unlikely to find fruit remains in their scat.

STOAT AND WEASEL

When found, the scat is very distinctive. It can often be extremely twisted and will often contain fur. The two species are very difficult to separate, except to say that extremely small scat is likely to be weasel and the larger scat will be stoat. There is, of course, a total crossover in size between the different sexes of these animals, which is reflected in the overlapping sizes of their scat.

I have found the extremely twisted scat of both species in latrines under reptile refugia and on top of log piles in which these creatures were living and hunting. The smell, in my experience, is unremarkable.

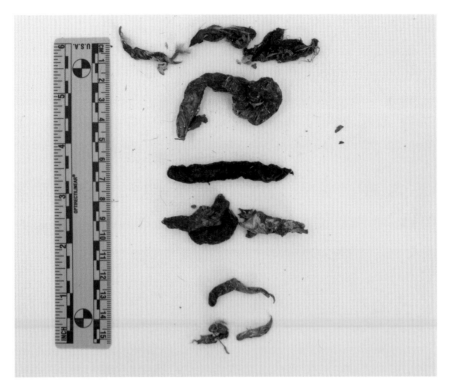

Mustelid scat (from the top): Otter, pine marten, American mink, polecat, stoat and weasel.

OTTER

I have put otters in this category as they are capable of producing long, tapering, twisted scat. However, it is frequently presented in small fragments and used for scent marking. In such cases, it often looks much smaller than one would expect from such a large animal. The scat can, in this form, be relatively shapeless and look almost smeared. It often contains fish bones, scales, crayfish parts and mammal fur.

Otters will revisit the same area to scat over and over again, and will pick places that are protected from the elements. Beneath overhangs and under bridges are great places to find otter scat of all ages, which is something I imagine you wouldn't have thought you'd be getting excited about.

The smell is, unsurprisingly, quite fishy but not especially unpleasant.

Otter spraint.

Otters often use a high point to mark with their spraint.

CLUMPS AND SPLATS

Scat in this category may be very typical for the particular species producing them or may be an occasional presentation from one of the species already covered. The cow pies, or pats, made by the numerous cows we find across our landscape are an often obvious and unmistakable part of any countryside walk in cattle country. They look like liquid mud and smell quite strong when fresh.

The obvious clump-producing animal is the horse, whose very fibrous scats can also be found almost everywhere in the countryside.

Above left: Cow pat.

Above right: Horse scat.

FOX AND BADGER

I have alluded to this already, but look out for fox and badger scat that can be very liquid, especially in the autumn when they are eating fruit. Also, when badgers have eaten a lot of earthworms their scat will resemble miniature cow pats.

Badger splat.

DEER

If ruminants such as deer eat moist and nutrient-rich vegetation their scat will become very liquid, look like miniature cow pats and will usually be very green inside. This can also happen earlier on in the year as the animals need time to build up gut bacteria as they switch from a dry, low nutrient winter food to the new, richer and wetter diet of fresh spring growth. It also occurs before the ruts as stags try their best to feed up before using lots of energy and through illness.

Roe deer loose scat.

Far left: Sometimes illness can also affect scat. This domestic dog has colitis.

Left: This domestic dog has a very loose scat, and a red fox has overmarked it.

BIRD SCAT

There are a few groups of birds that produce scat that could be mistaken for mammal scat. Birds generally produce scat that contains white uric acid and dark solid material. Unlike mammals, including ourselves, birds don't have separate openings for each deposit, and therefore it is mixed together in the opening technically known as the cloaca. There is variation in how, and how much of, each element is contained in the mix. Birds of prey and owls, in particular, produce scat with more uric acid than solids, as much of the solid material is regurgitated as a pellet (see below). In fact, their scat may sometimes be completely white. Raptors such as sparrowhawks and goshawks tend to shoot their scat out in a long line, while owls tend to drop it directly underneath themselves

Above left: Sparrowhawk scat.

Above right: Tawny owl scat.

Left: Pheasant scat found under a roost.

Woodpeckers, especially the green woodpecker, produce a scat with all of the uric acid on the outside of the dropping, coating an inner that comprises ant remains – ants being their staple diet. Large waterbirds, like geese, ducks and swans produce a classic 'j-shaped' scat with the uric acid forming a cap at the end of the dropping. With age, this cap often washes off, and the normally green body of the scat darkens, such that it can appear very mammal-like.

Pigeons generally produce a scat whorl like a Danish pastry, but diet can affect the colour, and impact (when dropped from a height) can squash it into all sorts of weird and wonderful shapes making it potentially confusing with other animals. The individual parts of the pigeon's whorl scat, dependant on diet, can look like tubes of mud and be mammal-like. When they feed on fruit, especially ivy berries, scat will be purple, and in a quantity that may be mistaken for sloppy marten scat.

I am hoping it will be possible to accurately identify more bird scat to species in the future. Work on this is an ongoing process.

Above: Woodpigeon scat after feeding on ivy berries.

Right: Green woodpecker scat filled with ant remains.

Above: Canada goose scat.

Above right: Pheasant caecal scat.

Bottom Right: Red grouse scat. (DW)

BIRD CAECAL DROPPINGS

All birds can produce this scat if needed, but birds that feed extensively on vegetation, such as game birds, produce it frequently. The caecum is responsible for breaking down coarse or fibrous vegetation with special-ised bacteria, and the resulting scat is very distinctive. Caecal scat may or may not have some of the white uric acid that frequently identifies scat as coming from a bird. Its colour will vary from light brown to black and, if broken (use a stick), it looks like melted chocolate. Presumably due to the powerful bacteria, this scat smells like the bottom of the worst-smelling chicken house you can imagine (hence the need for a stick). Sometimes it is in the form of obvious blobs, and occasionally it is longer and more sausage-like. I have had participants on CyberTracker evaluations, quite understandably, confuse it with carnivore droppings.

LIZARD

Lizard scat can look very much like bird droppings as they have similar mechanism for evacuation of their waste. These often have tapering scat with a white uric cap on the top.

Lizard scat.

PELLETS

All birds are capable of producing pellets, but some do it all of the time, with corvids, gulls, birds of prey and owls perhaps the most frequently encountered. Due to the variation in mammal scat, the pellets of birds of prey and owls can be confused with some of our carnivores, although with some experience they become only superficially scat-like. A pellet is the indigestible/undesirable part of a bird's meal that doesn't make it fully through the digestive system.

Perhaps the birds most people think of first when talking about pellets are owls, which are well known for catching small rodents and swallowing them whole. The regurgitated pellets contain the fur and bones of their prey and the presence of small bones is key to identification. The tiny bones of mice and voles do not readily survive in the digestive juices of carnivores.

If you find bones inside the scat of, say, a fox, they will undoubtedly be crunched fragments and large, such as those belonging to rabbits. If breaking open the suspected bird pellet reveals intact bones as small and delicate as the ribs and leg bones of voles or mice, then this will be an owl.

If there are lots of these small bones inside, it is further evidence of it being an owl and a not a similar-looking bird of prey pellet. An owl's digestion is relatively inefficient and their pellets (which are formed in the gizzard) may have up to ten times more small bones than the pellets of a bird of prey. Additionally, many birds of prey are much more likely to catch their prey, pluck it or pull it apart and then eat it, rather than swallowing it whole (as owls do), so the bones are less often consumed.

Distinguishing between the various species of owls purely from their pellets is less straightforward than many would have you believe, and both size and location becomes a key component to this process. Pellets of the

European eagle owl are huge and may contain bones as large as rabbit jaw bones. However, those of a little owl may contain beetle cases and lots of grass as they hunt for worms and bugs in parkland environments.

An owl pellet in a farm building is much more likely to be from a barn owl than a tawny owl, but they are of a very similar size, and the size varies considerably depending on how many prey items have been consumed. That said, I once walked through a woodland on three separate occasions and each time flushed a pair of barn owls from the same tree. The ground underneath was littered with pellets which, given the location, I would have said were tawny, had I not seen the birds. Barn owls are much less likely to be in this habitat. If I find good-sized pellets under a dense conifer or a tree covered in ivy then I would generally suspect tawny owl, as this is a perfect place for them to roost during the day away from the scolding of other birds.

Buzzard and red kite pellets are often found and, in my experience, look like owl pellets but with nothing or very little in the way of small bones in them. So, once again, location is important as both owl and raptor pellets are most likely to be found under places where they roost or perch regularly. Always bear in mind that there will be a crossover. For example, it is common for tawny owls to kill birds as big as pigeons, which they will clearly not be swallowing whole, in which case the resulting pellets may look entirely atypical.

Bird pellets. *Top row*: European eagle owl, barn owl and tawny owl. *Middle row*: Buzzard and kestrel. *Bottom row*: Little owl and jackdaw.

Above: Owl pellet opened to reveal field vole remains. (GH)

Right: Red kite pellet opened to reveal contents.

Above: Carrion crow pellet.

Left: Rook pellets seem to be much softer than other corvids.

CORVID PELLETS

Once again, the diet of these birds means the pellets will vary to some extent but, generally speaking, corvid pellets contain a large amount of vegetation such as dry grass stalks, grain husks and small stones. I have found them under fence posts where they perch – particularly true of carrion crows – and on top of ant hills in the middle of parkland where the culprits turned out to be jackdaws. Looking under rookeries will also often also yield results, although rook pellets do seem to be less solid than those of crows and jackdaws, and often distort as they hit the ground.

GULL PELLETS

The most obvious gull pellets will be found at coastal locations and will be filled with bits of broken seashell. These pellets are fairly soft and ephemeral and will soon disappear if exposed to the weather or waves.

Gull pellet (unknown species).

SIGNS ON TREES AND PLANTS

There are several reasons why an animal will damage vegetation, and exploring these reasons helps focus the mind to find the culprit. For example, considering exactly what an animal might want with a tree produces quite a short list. It could be either feeding, gathering materials, advertising itself, scratching an itch, causing incidental damage and so on. So, when confronted by sign, begin by asking yourself the question, 'What was the animal after?' It's a great starting point.

DAMAGE TO THE TRUNK AND BARK

ANTLER RUBS

Of our six species of deer, red, sika, fallow and roe regularly mark trees with their antlers. This action is often described as being done to remove the velvet from the antlers. Antler is essentially bone, and as it grows, the required blood supply is provided by the suede-like skin (the velvet) on the outside. Once antler growth is complete the blood supply is cut off and the velvet falls away, often to be eaten again by the deer or some other lucky creature – waste not want not!

There may be an element of this velvet removal in the purpose of antler rubs, but as this continues way past the point when the velvet has gone, it clearly isn't the whole story. Deer have scent glands between their antlers, and this perhaps explains a significant part of the antler-rubbing story. Scraping with the feet, and therefore scent marking with interdigital glands, is also often a part of this process, as is urinating next to the antler rub, and in some species even rolling in this urine. There is also an element of strength training as the animal pushes on a tree, simulating a fight with a rival male. And then there is the sheer frustration that goes with the deer finding itself suddenly full of testosterone.

Antler rubs can be identified as such by the damage going right down to the wood, and the frayed ends of remaining bark being torn vertically both up and down, which is very different to the cambium feeding described below. Depending on the species, the tree damage from rubs will be at a specific season and at a specific height.

Damage, with a few exceptions, doesn't occur outside of the period of time when the testicles of male deer descend. In the case of roe deer, they have a specific and interesting life cycle in that the bucks begin to set out territories in March/April and will scrape the ground and rub trees then. Sometimes, they scrape without marking trees, sometimes they scrape and mark, and sometimes they mark and don't scrape. The key point to this is that, should you find a fresh rub on a tree from spring to summer (the rut for roe deer is late summer), and the damage is concentrated at around knee height, it will be a roe deer.

There may also be damage lower, sometimes almost at ground level, and also higher, with some occasional antler strikes at the full extent that the animal can reach. When determining which animal did the damage, focus on where the bulk of the damage occurs. Also, consider the size of the rub. Roe deer, for example, often rub on quite small diameter trees and even thistles.

Antler rubs of the three larger species of deer can be difficult to separate from each other. They will all often beat up trees generally higher than a roe deer, of course, but separating red, sika and fallow damage may not be as straightforward. These animals can be of a similar size and therefore damage trees to similar heights. Local knowledge, other track and sign, and species range maps may be useful here.

All of these deer will damage trees of a larger diameter than roe generally do, but don't rely just on the size of the tree to reach a conclusion. I have seen roe deer damage on quite large-diameter trees, and fallow deer will destroy small trees and even plantation trees still in their plastic guards.

The season for this large deer activity will be centred around the autumn rut, which should eliminate roe deer from your list of suspects when working with fresh sign.

Of the other two deer species found in our region, Chinese water deer do not have antlers and so won't be found rubbing trees. I do not see antler rubbing by Reeves's muntjac with the same regularity as with the other species but do find territorial marking in the form of hoof scraping. They also scent mark with their large pre-orbital glands. When they do rub the damage will be centred at a height much lower than a roe deer. Both of these smaller species have enlarged canines, and it could be that they use these to mark trees, as indeed may larger species of deer that possess canines, such as red deer.

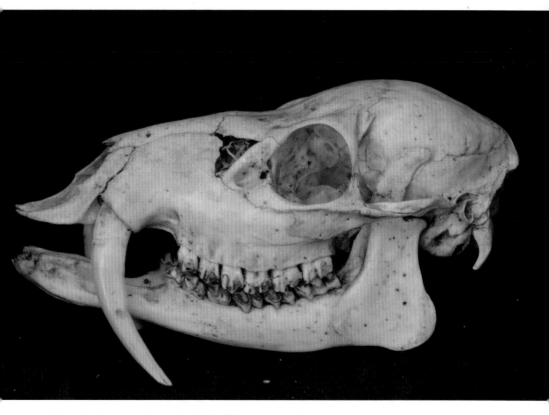

Note the large canine teeth of this Chinese water deer.

Above left: This fallow deer has destroyed the tree guard and damaged this young tree.

Above centre: Roe deer will often pick small rubbing posts.

Above right: Fallow deer rub on a Western red cedar.

FEEDING

A number of animals feed on tree bark, or more specifically, the inner bark or phloem layer which is packed full of sugars. This is the thin layer of material just under the outer bark and before the true wood starts. It is responsible for the movement of sugars around the tree and if it is removed all the way around the tree it may die. The main culprits for this behaviour are deer, rabbits and hares, squirrels and small rodents such as voles.

Often referred to as cambium feeding, this can occur in the spring or summer, but also the winter. Deer will take the inner bark at all times of year, but winter feeding, when there is less sap in the tree, is characterised by the removal of relatively small patches due to the inner bark being firmly attached to the tree at this time. There will also be clear evidence of incisor scrape marks which, in deer, will be large, as illustrated.

In the spring and summer, when there is a good deal of sap in the trees, the inner and outer bark can be pulled off in strips, leaving the smooth wood exposed and relatively free from incisor marks. With cambium feeding, the outer bark is also (for the most part) eaten, and the associated damage found with antler rub (such as frayed bark and antler strikes) will be absent.

If the sign is fairly fresh, it is also possible to see if the bark has been removed from the bottom and pulled up, indicating it was done by an ungulate. Ungulates (deer, sheep and goats, etc.) have incisors only in the lower jaw, and these dig into the bark at the bottom and the animal pulls up, tearing the bark away.

With summer barking, incisor marks are often to be seen on the tree where the tear started. All of our larger deer species regularly feed in this way. I have personally never found sign of roe deer doing this. Keep in mind that other larger animals, including horses, will also damage trees to get at the inner bark. Horses do have both upper and lower incisors, so won't necessarily create the same sign. For horses, look for diagonal incisor marks caused by both sets of incisors, and therefore damage from both directions. When trying to separate cambium feeding from antler rubbing, sometimes the location will help. Damage from feeding is often to be found in tight places where it would be impossible for a deer with a full set of antlers to get its head in and rub.

Note the lack of upper incisors on this sika deer and the vestigial canine tooth.

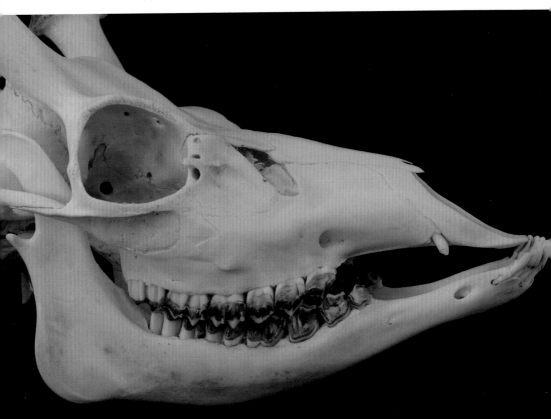

Above left: Cambium feeding by deer.

Above centre: Cambium feeding by horses.

Above right: Red deer incisor scraping.

Squirrels, rabbits and hares will also damage trees to get at the inner bark. In the case of squirrels, this can often be high up in the canopy where, if they remove the bark in a complete girdle, it will kill all parts of the tree above this point. Rabbits and hares generally focus their efforts lower down, although they will also stand on snow and walk along fallen trees to feed, which can lead to some confusion.

The incisor marks of squirrels are much smaller than ungulates, and they leave quite large chunks of outer bark behind as the focus is on scraping the cambium off the wood itself. Squirrels favour thin-barked trees, especially beech and sycamore.

Rabbits tend to leave much smaller fragments, if any, behind and there may also be associated signs of droppings nearby. Because of their upper and lower incisors, these animals cannot really pull the bark off in strips, even when it is loose on the tree.

The upper incisors of lagomorphs are notched and can leave characteristic lines when they feed; this may look like four smaller incisors in parallel lines. They also have a smaller extra pair of incisors set behind these main front ones, which may also help in identifying their skulls.

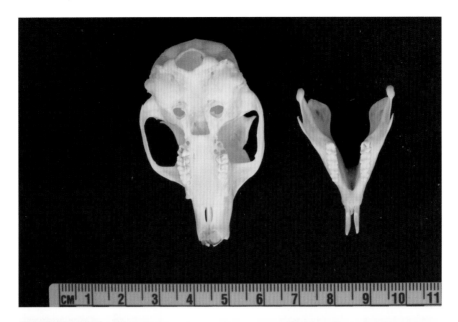

Grey squirrel incisors.

Above left: Grey squirrel incisor marks, in this case caused when gathering nesting material.

Above right: Grey squirrel feeding on a beech tree.

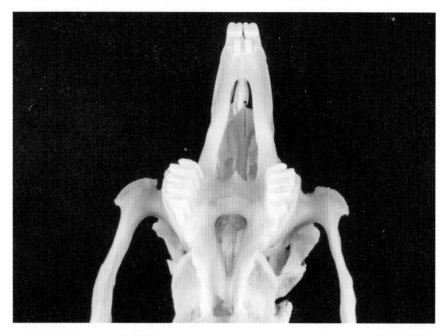

Upper incisors of a rabbit showing the additional vestigial teeth and the notch in the front teeth.

Sooty bark fungus harvested by small rodents.

Mice and voles target smaller trees, and usually around the base. Their incisors are much smaller and leave very fine lines compared to the other animal groups. Like squirrels, though, they leave bits of outer bark behind, although in much smaller-sized chunks. They will often target trees which are contained within tree guards and, in the case of bank voles, will also climb to target branches.

Increasingly, in our landscape, it is also possible to find the sign of beaver cambium feeding, and the felling of entire trees.

I have noticed other feeding phenomena on a dead sycamore killed by sooty bark disease (*Cryptostroma corticale*), which is a type of fungi that leaves a distinctive black coating on the dead stems. I have found this fungus many times in conjunction with tiny incisor marks, that are frequent and close enough together to indicate that the culprit is scraping off the fungi and eating it. For years, I was wondering what had caused this until, on a dead, horizontal stem, I found bank vole scat in conjunction with the feeding sign. All that can be concluded from this is that bank voles eat the fungi, and it is possible that other small rodents may take advantage. Bank voles will also climb higher into the trees and strip smaller twigs, presumably targeting areas where the outer bark is thin.

Like rabbits and squirrels, water voles and field voles are capable of completely ring-barking a tree by removing bark from its entire circumference, effectively killing it. There may also be an element of nest gathering from the inner bark as I have also found squirrel incisor marks in the same locations.

As is well known, beavers fell trees and strip bark for a number of reasons, using trees and branches to construct dams and lodges, but also feeding on the bark and even storing this for use in the winter. Their activities are unmistakable, with often quite large trees felled, leaving behind a characteristic gnawed tree stump surrounded by big wood chips that nothing else in the UK could really produce. Beaver incisors leave extremely wide furrows when they strip bark. They often scent mark the stumps they have felled, from a gland close to their anus. I experienced this once in Poland when I put my hand on a scent-marked stump – my, that scent did linger.

A beaver can take down surprisingly big trees.

Left: Tree felled by beaver. (DW)

Right: A stick that has been crosscut by a beaver.

Beavers collect lots of sticks to build lodges and dams.

Above left: The beaver is so powerful it can remove large chunks of wood with its incisors.

Above right: I am not sure if the deer pushed this tree over or if the wind uprooted it, but they have targeted the upper branches as food.

BREAKING TREES

Trees tend to produce less of the bitter-tasting anti-browse chemicals higher up in the stem as there is no need to waste energy making them if the chief browsers can't reach. Look out for trees that have broken or blown over after storms, as the browsing animals will target the branches closest to the top. (Incidentally, holly has a similar strategy and will often produce leaves without prickles higher in the canopy.) Deer will often push small trees down to reach the top, effectively holding the stems under their chest. Roe deer do this fairly commonly, while Reeves's muntjac will break small trees and saplings to solve the same problem.

BODY RUBS

Several species of animal may rub trees as part of scratching, scent marking, or just from being around a tree for a long period of time. The most likely encountered rubs are from wild boar, badgers, horses and other domestic animals.

Above left: Tree regularly used as a scratching post by badgers.

Above right: This wild boar rubbing tree was adjacent to a wallow.

Red deer have rubbed on this resinous conifer – note the hair.

Wild boar rubs are frequently associated with mud. These animals will leave a mud wallow and then immediately find a tree to rub against. They may also damage the tree quite severely with their tusks and leave hair stuck to the tree with the mud. The wallow is often seen quite close by, and the height of the rub is relatively low when compared to a deer rub, for example. Often a resinous tree species is chosen, and they may mark these trees with their prominent tusks.

The larger species of deer will rub trees in the same way as wild boar, and frequently in conjunction with a wallow. This may be in done as part of the rut, but females will also rub on trees. I have found evidence of red deer rubbing on resinous trees just as wild boar do.

Badgers will rub on trees really, I believe, just to scratch themselves. I have witnessed this very behaviour on many occasions. Hair can often be found associated with obviously smoothed bark (suggesting a regularly visited scratching tree), along with some mud. Badgers will also occasionally leave claw marks on trees.

Horses and other domestic animals, including cows and sheep, will also rub trees, especially in areas where they congregate for shade or shelter.

Seeing the tusks on the wild boar makes it easy to envisage the damage they can do to trees.

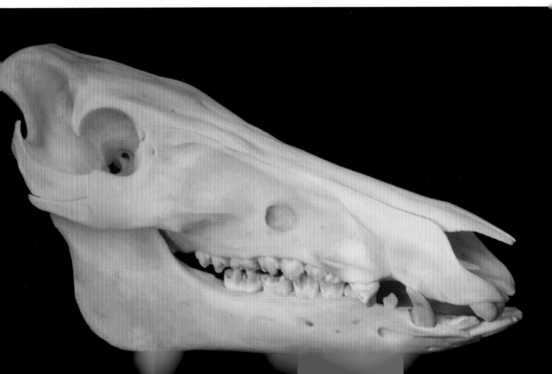

STRIPING

Both our species of squirrel are known for marking trees vertically up and down the trunk, but also horizontally along the branches. This can be on either dead wood or a living tree and is known as striping. The outermost layer of weathered bark is removed with the teeth and is then rubbed over with scent from glands in the cheeks. This is not a territorial sign but serves to let all the local squirrels who is about in the neighbourhood. On tree trunks, it is often found on the leeside and/or under the lean of the tree, presumably to protect the scent from weathering. I have even found it on the edges of posts.

Above: Grey squirrel striping on a sweet chestnut.

Right: This post has been used by a grey squirrel to scent mark.

Above left: Outer bark harvested for nesting material.

Above right: Inner bark harvested for nesting. Note the incisor marks of the grey squirrel.

NESTING

Many rodents gather dead inner bark and the outer bark of trees to use as nesting materials. Squirrels are particularly keen on this and will visit trees repeatedly, causing a huge amount of sign and leaving thick-barked trees like Western red cedar looking quite chewed up, although in tree species like this it is the fibrous outer bark they focus on. The impact can look dramatic, but the tree is either dead already (when the inner bark is targeted) or only the outer bark is removed, leaving the vital phloem intact (as with the Western red cedar example).

Small rodents will also target the dead inner bark from trees such as sycamore for nesting, as well as the outer bark of climbers like honey-suckle and clematis. Honeysuckle is a well-loved favourite of the hazel dormouse. Squirrels will also take the inner bark layer for food and may girdle the tree and ring-bark it. This kills the tree from the point above this damage.

This root was debarked by horses' hooves.

HOOVES

Exposed tree roots may be damaged through feeding, as described above, or from the action of hard-hooved animals walking across them.

SCRATCHES

Trees and logs can be scratched simply by the regular passage of animals along or over them, or more deliberately. Both cats (including wildcat) and badgers will regularly reach up and rake trees with their claws, and recently badgers have been filmed climbing trees, which will also leave signs. Very fine scratches can also be found, particularly on smooth-barked trees, from the claws of squirrels and pine martens

Badger claw marks on a log across a regular travel route. The bark has been removed, revealing some bark beetle breeding galleries.

Above left: Cat using a fence post regularly, but this damage also occurs on trees. (DC)

Above right: Squirrel claw marks.

Mechanical damage caused timber felling and extraction along this track.

MECHANICAL DAMAGE

This type of damage can be caused by mowers, strimmers and flails; felled trees being dragged into standing trees when timber is extracted; wind-blown trees hitting standing trees; and even lightning strikes. It can sometimes be difficult to separate this mechanical damage from animal sign.

WOODPECKER FEEDING

Holes in dead wood, if crisp-edged and perfectly round or oval, are likely to be the exit (or emergence) holes of wood-boring beetles. The oval holes are most probably those of longhorn beetles (a specific group of wood borer) and the round ones will be insects such as bark or ambrosia beetles. Holes that are very ragged at the edges are likely to be woodpecker feeding sign, made in search of the beetle larvae before they emerge. The commonest culprit leaving such sign in the UK is the great spotted woodpecker.

SAP WELLS

Great spotted woodpeckers will also create sap wells in the bark of the tree. These wells don't penetrate deeply into the wood, just far enough to reach the phloem. The purpose of these holes is to draw sap, which is then either drunk, left to attract insects (which are then eaten), or both. Most of this distinctive damage seems to occur in the early spring when there are few insects about, suggesting that the birds are either just going for the sap, or luring some fairly specialist early emergent insects as a long-awaited protein fix.

WOODPECKER NEST HOLES

Woodpeckers characteristically excavate holes in trees in which to raise their young. These holes are often later taken over by other birds or mammals.

Right: The ragged feeding hole of a great spotted woodpecker.

Below left: Oval exit hole, most likely for a long-horn beetle.

Below right: Round hole, most likely made by a bark or ambrosia beetle.

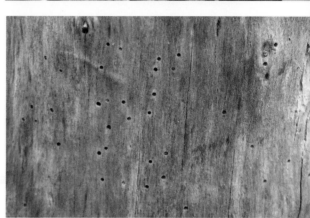

Above left: Sap wells on a lime tree caused by a great spotted woodpecker.

Above centre: Weeping sap well. (DW)

Above right: Woodpecker nest hole.

Left: Slug feeding on the algae on the side of a trailer.

Below: Log that has been broken open by a badger.

SLUGS

Slugs leave very distinctive feeding marks on the algae that grows on trees. Slugs have a structure called a radula that they use for feeding. It is ribbon-like and covered in 27,000 teeth. This radula scrapes away at their food, leaving a very distinctive curved feeding pattern on anything they eat, which can be algae, but also a good deal of fungi when these are available.

ROTTEN LOGS

Badgers in particular, but also woodpeckers, will break open rotten logs to access the larvae of wood-boring insects contained within.

FEEDING ON TWIGS AND HERBACEOUS PLANTS

The way that stems and twigs of all kinds are harvested gives us big clues as to who did the harvesting. Deer, as previously mentioned, only have incisors in the lower jaw and a hard palate in the upper. They will invariably leave a ragged edge on any nibbled shoots as they cannot scissor two sets of teeth together to make a clean cut. They will similarly leave ragged edges on grasses and other herbaceous plants they harvest. Deer are true browsers and will wander about nipping the tops out of young trees (much to the annoyance of foresters), and anything else that takes their fancy. They especially like roses (much to the annoyance of gardeners), and other woodland plants in the rose family like bramble. Although deer have their favourites, look for their sign on pretty much anything from ivy to bluebells.

A lot is written about the height of damage to identify deer but do be aware that red deer are well known to stand on their hind legs to reach higher branches, and I have seen Reeves's muntjac do this too, so I assume the other deer species can all do this.

Deer browse line.

225

Above left: Deer leave a ragged end when feeding.

Above right: Roe deer feeding on dandelions. The central rib proved too tough for one set of incisors

In areas of high deer concentrations (or other browsers, such as cows and horses), the trees will often show a 'browse line' caused by the animals repeatedly nibbling the lower branches of the trees.

Look out for deer browsing the broader leaves of some of our native herbaceous plants. They regularly harvest the very tips of the leaves of docks and primroses, leaving a distinctive bite profile, or sometimes a ragged tear. I have also witnessed deer targeting plants which are known to be quite toxic and/or medicinal, and I am sure there is some self-medication aspect to this behaviour.

Small stems cut neatly at 45 degrees are the work of rodents using their upper and lower incisors to cut like scissors. Identification can be tricky but prime suspects include field voles and water voles, who often cut stems into neat lengths that can then be found in tidy piles. In the case of field voles, these piles can be in their runs, and in the case of water voles, it is usually bigger-stemmed material close to water, although there is a crossover in both habitat and the size of the material handled.

Rabbits and hares also cut cleanly but can do it higher up the stem and therefore their feeding can be confused with deer. Telling rabbits and hares apart using this sign alone is a little more difficult, and it is not always possible to be certain.

Water vole feeding sign.

Above left: Evidence of the feeding activities of a water vole – note the gnawed plant fragments.

Above right: Remains of field vole feeding.

Left: This is an old feeding station of a field vole.

The neatly clipped ends that signify lagomorph feeding sign. This is old but it makes the sign easier to see.

Above left: This crop has been pushed over by a badger.

Above right: Woodpigeons feeding on chard.

Badgers frequently push down cereal crops, especially in dry summers, when they struggle to dig down to their favourite food of worms. They target the ears of grain and consequently produce an interesting range of granola-like scat in their latrines.

Woodpigeons, in particular, will tear up the leaves of plants to eat agricultural crops or your garden vegetables, often eating these down to the ground. Plants can be left with a characteristic ripped-up appearance.

INSECTS

There are a plethora of insect species that damage vegetation in all kinds of varied and interesting ways. Sometimes, it is the action of feeding by either the adults or their young that causes the damage, most noticeably on leaves. With other species, the action of laying eggs and the resulting larvae will cause plant cells to deform and create weird and wonderful shapes, as is the case with galls. The study of insect sign could take a lifetime, so here I only include the ones most often encountered.

Above left: Hazel big bud gall mite, *Phytoptus avellanae.*

Above right: Nut leaf blister moth, *Phyllonorycter coryli.*

Above left: Unknown long-horn beetle larval case.

Above right: Many insects cause raised galls on the leaves and stems of plants and trees like this alder gall mite, *Eriophyes laevis*.

Robin's pin cushion gall wasp (*Diplolepis rosae*) – some galls can be quite beautiful.

Above left: Wasp, paper making.

Above right: Oak apple gall wasp, *Biorhiza pallida.*

Right: Marble gall wasp, *Andricus kollari.*

Below left: A leaf cutter bee in action. (GH)

Below right: Distinct damage left by the leaf cutter bee. (GH)

SIGNS ON NUTS, SEEDS, FRUIT AND FUNGI

A wide range of creatures like to join in and harvest the seasonal bounty produced through the reproductive efforts of plants, trees and fungi. This is a huge subject in terms of animal sign with many aspects of it still to be discovered, or at least recorded.

NUTS AND SEEDS

Many creatures are attracted to nuts as a food source, ranging from insects through birds and mammals of all sizes. Occasionally, mammals are attracted to the small insects within a nut, as is the case with grey squirrels seeking acorn weevils. In late summer, unripe, green acorns are often found, obviously opened but with the flesh discarded, as the squirrel will harvest the weevil grub and discard the unripe flesh of the acorn.

Grey squirrels are also renowned for opening hazelnuts before they ripen, but this has nothing to do with a search for grubs. Characteristically, squirrel-opened nuts are split cleanly in half. There are few, if any, scratch marks left on a nut opened by a grey squirrel. Occasionally, there may be marks where the animal has struggled for purchase, and a little notch on the half where its incisors have managed to locate, but they are clean other than this. Even if the animal struggles with this task and opens the nut in a less than tidy fashion, the shell is

This acorn has been opened by a grey squirrel to access weevil grubs.

Hazelnut that has been split cleanly by a grey squirrel.

Even when the nut is not split evenly, the strength of the grey squirrel's jaws is evident in the centre nut in this photo.

effectively ripped open. I imagine it like the animal just popping the lid of the biscuit tin, their jaws are that powerful.

There is another creature that splits open hard seeds (such as cherry stones and hornbeam seeds) in a similar manner, the hawfinch. You may find the split shells of these seeds underneath the trees they've been feeding in. It is likely that birds such as greenfinches may also open hard seeds in a similar way.

Seed on the side of a tree, most likely split by a hawfinch.

NUTS WITH HOLES

Hard nuts like hazelnuts are important food sources for many small mammals other than squirrels. Wood and yellow-necked mice, bank voles and hazel dormice all open nuts in a specific and identifiable way.

Both bank voles and mice leave a chiselled edge at the rim of the hole they create. Imagine a miniature mallet and chisel chipping away from the edge of the nut towards the centre of the hole itself. In effect, this is how the tiny teeth chisel away to break into the nut.

The difference between these groups of animals is that mice scratch up the area close to the edge of the rim with their incisors, and bank voles do not. This scratching is termed 'chatter' and is caused because the mice, once they have broken into the nut, gnaw at the far side of the opening, marking the 'varnish' of the shell with their upper incisors. This technique has the mice feeding with their noses outside of the hole they're making. In contrast, bank voles, once they have created an opening, gnaw at the side closest to themselves with their noses inside the hole.

Hazel dormice do a similar thing to the mice and leave chatter, but instead of producing neat little chisel marks on the rim of the hole, they create a groove that spirals around the rim of the hole. These animals often leave the same marks on hawthorn and cherry stones, which they open in the same way.

Above left: Hazelnut that has been opened by a hazel dormouse.

Above centre: Hazelnut that has been opened by a wood or yellow-necked mouse.

Above right: Hazelnut that has been opened by a bank vole.

Above left: Bank vole cache in an old tree guard.

Above right: A grey squirrel feeding table.

Left: Remains after grey squirrels have been feeding in the canopy.

Location can also help with the identification of feeding remains from small rodents. Mice and voles tend to cache nuts for the winter, which can often be found in holes in trees, bird boxes, etc. The tracker is often alerted to these caches as the animals throw out the empties. Day-to-day feeding is also carried out under the cover of boards, tins, logs or amongst tree roots – indeed, anywhere they are safe from predators such as owls.

Hazel dormice tend not to feed on the ground, so their empty nut shells are normally scattered more randomly as they fall from the trees. Squirrels also feed in the canopy, and sometimes litter the floor with the remains of their meals. If they feed on the ground, they try to select a high spot, known as a table, and use it repeatedly, such that it may build up an impressive midden of empty shells. The table can be anything from a fallen tree, a tree stump or even a mole hill.

PEELED NUTS

Chestnuts and acorns have much softer shells than nuts and seeds like cherry and hazel, but it is still possible to use similar criteria to establish who has opened them. It is harder to separate bank vole and the mice species, but squirrels tend to pull big chunks off and are quite messy feeders. Also, the location is the same in terms of where you will find them. Wild boar and deer will also eat these types of soft nuts, and often leave the shell behind as a clue.

Chestnuts and acorns are opened by a number of birds, most typically corvids, which tend to hold them down and stab at them with their bill. I have found them in little divots in the ground (as shown), presumably used like a temporary anvil.

Cones have nutritious nuts at the base of each of the scales and so are sought after by the rodents mentioned above. Their sign can be separated into rough mammal groups, again using location and also how neat the work is. Squirrels leave quite ragged bits of the scales of pine and spruce cones attached to the main stem. Smaller rodents, by comparison, are able to eat right down to the stem, leaving a much neater finish. Some scales are often left attached, presumably because they are empty of nuts or unripe.

The great spotted woodpecker is a keen exploiter of cones and will most often create a spot in a tree or, as I have seen, in a telegraph pole, that exactly fits its meal. It will use this over and over again, and the location of such anvils is often given away by the pile of discarded cones at its base. Woodpeckers will do this with nuts as well as cones. Larger cones may be hammered on the floor in a similar way as corvids do with chestnuts. In fact, it is probable that corvids also open pine cones in this way, although I have not witnessed it myself.

Characteristically, when birds with pickaxe-like bills (woodpeckers, corvids, nuthatch) open cones, there is a great deal of impact and forcing apart of the scales.

Nuthatches do a similar thing with hazelnuts and a variety of other cones and hard seeds, but instead of making a purpose built anvil, they find a suitable crevice in the bark of tree, such as an oak, and without modification they wedge their meal in. This sign is revealed by the nut still being present and no empty nuts beneath the tree as they are a single-use feature.

Above left: I witnessed a jackdaw hammering this chestnut with its bill. I presume the crevice in the ground was selected deliberately as an anvil to hold it still.

Above right: Cones handled by a grey squirrel (the two on the left) and a small rodent (on the right).

Above left: Great spotted woodpecker anvil.

Above right: Cones that have been opened by a great spotted woodpecker.

Crossbills have a slightly different strategy for dealing with cones, using their specially adapted crossed bill to twist and prise the scale away from the body of the cone, exposing the nut at the base. This leaves a ragged appearance but with scales still attached to the main body of the cone. This action often splits the cone scales lengthways.

Above: Nuthatch workstation in a bark crevice of an oak.

Right: Larch cone opened by a crossbill.

An apple that has been cleaned out by a Blackbird.

FRUITS

Fruits of all sizes are eaten by mammals as big as deer and wild boar, although most likely even things as big as apples are usually completely consumed by these larger animals, leaving nothing for the tracker to find. Larger fruits will be fed upon by the larva of insects and adult wasps. Birds (blackbirds and other thrushes, in particular) often eat out the flesh of fallen apples, characteristically leaving only the skin behind.

Small fruits eaten by larger animals such as foxes can later be found in their scat. I have found hawthorn, blackberry, cherry and yew seed in fox and badger droppings (see the section on scat).

When small rodents eat fruits, what is left behind can be a clue as to who was feasting. Voles and hazel dormice tend to leave the seeds behind while mice target the seeds and often leave the flesh. This is also true of birds that will peck out the seed from fruits like rosehips and leave behind the flesh.

Above: These cherries were defleshed by squirrels and the stones dropped under the tree.

Left: Dandelion seed that has been harvested by goldfinches.

Many birds do a similar thing, in fact, some plant species rely on this pref-erence. The mistle thrush helps 'plant' mistletoe seeds on branches. It does this by favouring the flesh over the seed and then wiping its beak on a convenient branch, leaving the seed behind to germinate and latch on to the tree.

Fine seeds of thistles and dandelions may also be harvested by gold-finches, linnets and other small finches.

FUNGI

Fungi are consumed by wild boar, deer, squirrels, small rodents and insects, as well as slugs. Wild boar and deer often eat them whole, although I have found the poisonous panther cap fungi nibbled by sika deer. Just one piece was taken, which does make me wonder if there was an element of self-medication involved. Many medicinal chemicals are poisonous in high quantities, but animals are known to seek out nature's pharmacy, taking small quantities as needed.

Above: Small rodent incisor marks on hedgehog fungi.

Left: Amanita that has been nibbled by sika deer.

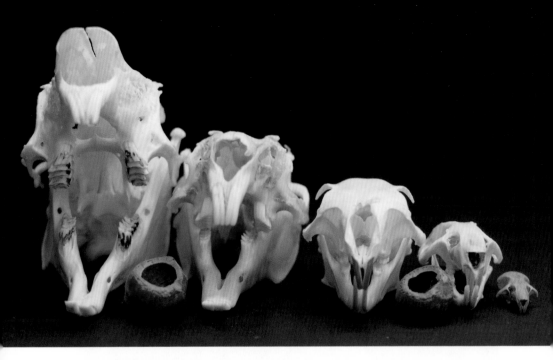

It is worth becoming familiar with the relative sizes of the incisors of various animals to match them with any damage found. Left to right: hare, rabbit, squirrel, brown rat and bank vole with vole-opened hazelnut for scale

Slug feeding on a dryad's saddle.

Squirrels and small rodents are best separated by the size of the incisor marks left on the fungi. It is worth getting to grips with these incisor mark differences, as the animals in question leave their teeth marks on all sorts of surfaces.

The most common invertebrate feeding sign left on fungi is that of slugs, whose radula (and arcing head movement) leaves a distinctive circular, scooped pattern.

CORN

Sweet corn is often gown in the UK as a game bird cover crop, and the cobs are frequently found in the woodlands either partially or fully eaten. This is the work of pheasants, which often drag the cobs under the canopy for some protection while they eat.

Pheasant feeding on sweetcorn.

HOLES, NESTS AND PATHS

This section looks primarily at mammal homes, and only really refers to the dwellings of other creatures that may look similar. The identification of bird nests is a huge topic to cover and beyond the scope of this book. There are already splendid works on this subject which can be referred to.

HOLES

Very small holes are the work of insects and identifying this sign to species level can be quite difficult. There are a few guidelines that can hopefully help to narrow down the identification process. As described elsewhere in this book under a variety of subjects, the smaller the feet of the creature moving earth, generally speaking, the smaller are the pieces of earth produced and moved.

Holes with the width of a pencil or little finger in the centre of a miniature 'molehill' that's made up of quite course lumps of earth are most likely to be the work of dung beetles. Mammal scat is also often found close by, and the insects are in the process of dragging it down the hole as a food store for their larvae. As far as insects go, dung beetles have quite big feet, so their spoil is quite lumpy.

Solitary bees also produce a volcano of earth with a central hole. The spoil from these is much finer. Size will depend very much on species, with tawny mining bees, for example, leaving quite large diameter holes similar to those of the beetle. By contrast, polymorphic sweat bees are much smaller, leaving a hole no wider than a matchstick. Although these creatures are solitary, some species seem to form loose colonies. It may be that once a suitable area of ground for excavation has been discovered, everybody moves in. Whatever the reason, once one bee mound is found, there will often be many more in the vicinity.

Solitary wasps also dig holes in the ground but generally seem to burrow in at an angle, unlike dung beetles and bees, which tend to create vertical shafts.

Above left: Colonial nesting of polymorphic sweat bees. Note the very fine granular spoil produced.

Above right: Larger nest hole with coarser spoil of Andrena mining bee species. (SM)

Dung beetle at work.

Above left: Dung beetle mound and hole.

Above right: Burrow of a beewolf.

Left Meadow ant nest that has been opened by a green woodpecker.

Some species of ants also produce little mounds of spoil, particularly when the colonies are first started. Some of these may eventually grow into huge structures. Wood ants are a prime example of this. They create huge nests made primarily of leaf litter. These nests have small entrances which also help to cool and ventilate the mound. Incidentally, these wood ant mounds are usually asymmetrical, with the longer, gentler slope on the south side where it catches the most sun on its larger surface area.

Yellow meadow ants make nests that eventually cover with vegetation and become like little couches that can be sat on. They are a sign of ancient pasture as they do not survive the plough. Green woodpeckers often excavate ant hills to prey on the inhabitants.

Other small holes may be bird probe holes as they search out invertebrates. These are often obvious on the beach where wading birds have been feeding but can also be found in land made by birds such as the green woodpecker.

Left: Wood ant nest. Note the longer slope towards the camera, the southern side.

Below left: Green woodpecker probe holes.

Below right: Green woodpecker feeding hole in wood ant nest.

I classify mammal holes in several ways. Firstly, by size, with these approximate size classes: golf ball size, tennis ball size, grapefruit size, and anything bigger than these. Secondly, the size and position of the throw or indeed the presence or absence of spoil from the excavation. Some of these characteristics have already been alluded to in the section on digs. It is also worth considering any paths and runs entering and exiting the hole, and the width and shape of these.

SMALLER HOLES

These golf ball sized holes are most likely to be the work of voles and mice. I carried out a lot of work to establish who makes these commonly found small holes. Location can help; for example, a vole hole deep in woodland is less likely to be field vole and more likely to be bank vole.

I've placed trail cameras on numerous holes and found that the yellow-necked mouse generally produces much more spoil from digging than does the wood mouse. However, if there is just a small amount of soil outside the hole, it could be either species. If there is a lot, say a molehill sized amount, I lean towards a yellow-necked mouse. With either species, unlike moles, the hole is on the edge of the earth that is thrown out, which forms the shape of a fan. The entrance to a mole burrow is always in the centre of the mound. Fresh yellow-necked mouse digging activity is particularly evident in early spring

Bank voles tend not to produce earth outside of their hole, so a golf ball sized hole in woodland, without any spoil outside, is likely to be this creature. Voles tend to burrow in and then push the soil up on their backs to make progress. Mice are much more likely to dig and excavate the soil properly.

Field vole holes.

Above left: A bank vole burrow. Note the lack of spoil.

Above right: The amount of spoil from this small burrow is suggestive of a yellow-necked mouse.

Field voles make similar-sized holes in grass and vegetation and have runs and tunnels in the tight-knitted mat of thatch and roots at the base of grasses. It is not impossible to find field vole homes in woodland, especially if in wide, grassy woodland rides.

Another similar-sized hole you may come across, particularly in sandy environments such as heathland, are the test burrows of sand lizards. Females often dig these to assess the temperature and general suitability before they lay their eggs. If the environment is unsuitable, they do not fill them in. This results in a hole a little smaller, in fact, than a golf ball but with a flat bottom and arched roof, looking a little like a miniature badger hole.

Holes as big as a tennis ball match those made by brown rats and water voles. Similar distinctions apply, as described above, in that you are much more likely to find earth and all kinds of debris pushed out of the rat hole than that of a water vole.

The most likely candidate for a grapefruit sized hole is a rabbit. These are mostly colonial creatures, and this should be a good clue in identification. There is often also evidence in the form of scat and scrapes close by, as well as pieces of fur during the breeding season.

Do be aware that the burrows of rodents and rabbits are frequently taken over by appropriately sized members of the weasel family. Small rodent holes are also often colonised by bumblebees.

Mole holes are usually obvious from the huge amount of soil produced by these animals. However, this soil can get kicked around and flattened and make confusing sign consisting of a flattened, bare circle of earth with a hole in the centre of it. This happens regularly as mole runs often cross well-used footpaths. Look in the surrounding area for more holes. Size-wise, the holes themselves are a little bigger than mouse burrows, but not quite as big as rats. Periodically moles produce an extra big mound, known as a fortress, which contains a nest lined with vegetation and a food store of decapitated insects.

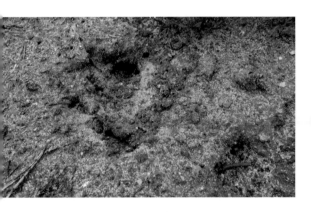

Above: Sand lizard test burrow.

Right: Brown rat hole.

Above: Mole hill – the hole is always in the centre of the mound but normally not visible.

Left: Rabbit hole.

BIG HOLES

Bigger holes, such as those made by badgers, are usually fairly easy to identify and are described in the section on digs and scrapes. Badgers can articulate their front paws outwards, which may lead to scratch marks also on the sides of the holes, instead of just the base. Generally speaking, badger holes look like the letter 'D' tilted on its side. The flat bottom of the badger hole matches the animal's profile of being wide-bodied but low to the ground. You may also find associated evidence of their paths which are distinctive.

The spoil heap in front of the hole is usually quite extensive, and you can often find traces of bedding material here and in the entrance. Badgers can also move surprisingly heavy lumps of material and may dig latrines and rub trees in the vicinity of their sett.

Something of interest regarding badger holes is the number of different types of sett they make, which was first pointed out to me by my friend and ecologist, Richard Andrews. Badgers have a main sett that is occupied all year round by the clan (normally comprising family members) and is used for breeding by the dominant male and female. They also often have an annexe sett close by, and well connected by travel routes to the main sett. They then have subsidiary setts, which may be used seasonally and are not as obviously connected by well-used paths to the other setts but are within the territory

Above left: A classic badger hole.

Above right: There are often extensive spoil mounds from badger digging.

Badger setts are often visible from a long way off.

Above left: Red fox holes are much less 'D'-shaped than badgers'. The foot-worn channel is also narrow by comparison.

Above right: This area shows the extensive flattening made by red fox cubs playing. There were numerous bird and animal remains in the immediate vicinity.

of the same clan of badgers. Finally, they have outlier setts that are only used occasionally as a kind of 'crash pad'. At certain times, they may not even rest underground and will use hollow trees or other secluded places.

Foxes dig a rounder hole, less D-shaped than the badger. In an active fox earth, there is often a pungent smell, and the remains of prey, including feathers, bones and skulls scattered around outside. If cubs are in residence, there is also a good deal of flattening caused by their play.

Location of a wildcat den. (Scottish Wildcat Action)

Evidence, in both cases, that the holes are active can often be found with fresh excavations, tracks in the spoil heaps, and the presence of flies around the holes. Very occasionally, in cold weather, I have seen steam rising from the entrance of badger setts as the animals' breath condenses.

Many animals just make dens in existing places like log piles and piles of rocks. Stoats and weasels do this, as do wild and feral cats.

NESTS

A large number of mammals create nests to rear their young. Some are seldom seen, being located in the depths of tunnel systems. Others, however, are surprisingly easily found and can be identified.

The largest, most conspicuous and most commonly found are the drays of squirrels. At first glance, they could be confused with a bird's nest, but they are normally located in the crook of the tree against the main trunk. They are oval in shape and made of sticks and are thick with leaves. The only common bird to make a nest of this shape would be a magpie, who builds a roof over its otherwise bowl-shaped nest, making it look dray-like, although the nest is almost entirely made of sticks and twigs. Big nests of birds of prey and other (non-magpie) corvids are less oval shaped and are much wider than they are high. Also look for leaves that make up part of the structure of a dray but are less prominent in bird nests of this size. General debris and leaf build-up in tree forks can be mistaken for a squirrel home.

Above: Grey squirrel dray.

Left: A half-finished magpie nest with roof visible.

Above left: A buzzard's nest has a much flatter platform than a grey squirrel's dray.

Above right: Bank vole nest found under paving slab.

Above left: Mouse nest made of leaves, found under a board.

Above right: Finely shredded material typical of vole nests.

Below left: A mouse nest in a hazel dormouse box, most likely belonging to a yellow-necked mouse.

Below right: Hazel dormouse nest.

Vole and mouse nests are made in tunnels but can also be found by lifting up logs, boards, paving slabs and, in the case of mice, even boxes in a loft or garage. Both field vole and bank vole make their nests of very finely shredded material, with tree bark and grasses being a favourite. Our mouse species tend towards a much coarser arrangement and regularly bring in dead leaves and bits of plastic and paper.

Hazel dormice build two kinds of nest. Their summer one is quite big and elaborate and made up of tree bark, especially the outer bark of honeysuckle and, characteristically, green leaves. With a little practice, it is easy to identify leaves that were gathered green and then dried and those, as in the case of mice, that were gathered already dead. Hazel dormouse summer nests are located off the ground in shrubby growth. The dormouse also builds a hibernation nest which is sometimes found on the ground in the buttress roots of trees (at least, that is where I have come across them).

The harvest mouse builds a tennis ball sized nest of woven grasses and leaves off the ground. The ones I have found have all been in bramble thickets, but they are also found woven into the stems of clump-forming grasses, cereal crops and reeds. Like the dormouse, they will also build a winter nest on the ground.

Above left: Hazel dormouse hibernation nest.

Above right: Harvest mouse nest.

Above: Hedgehog nest.

Right: Ball of grass dropped on a badger path –
note also the trail of grass along the travel route.

Hedgehogs also build nests, which are made up of grass, plant debris and dry, dead leaves. The ones I have found have been under other objects. The one illustrated was under an empty sandbag in my greenhouse and had young in it. Their hibernation nest is very similar and located in similar places. Leaving out piles of branches and leaves or building purpose-made homes for them can greatly help this declining species.

Also look out for badger nesting materials, which can frequently be found dropped along their trails. Evidence of these creatures gathering up leaf litter to take home to their sett is also a common sight.

PATHS AND RUNS

It is worth talking about the trails that animals take to get to their burrows and homes as these can be distinctive and lead the tracker naturalist to the animal. Some of these routes become well established and may even be centuries old. This is certainly true in the case of badgers.

Although one species may well begin to make a path, many others will take advantage of this route of least resistance. So, in some instances it is only possible to identify the prime user or the architect of a particular animal road.

Badger trails are very distinctive. Imagine a low-slung animal close to the ground going over and over the same route on a regular basis. The animal's paws compact and smooth down the soil at the same time as brushing leaf debris clear. The resulting trail is cleared to around 20cm in width.

Deer also use regular travel routes. Generally speaking, these much more delicate animals with longer, slender legs do not brush the ground clear in the same way as badgers. However, some of the bigger species, on regular routes known as racks, can create highways through the woods. Look for chopped-up substrate at pinch points (or bottlenecks) and where animals cross from one woodland to another.

Trails in the grass also lead to rabbits and rabbit feeding areas or, often, to the nest of a pheasant. If you're really lucky, you may find runs and slides into water made by beavers or otters.

Above left: Beaver trail in the snow.

Above right: Beaver exit point in mud. (DW)

Sometimes, the soil around the entrance of an animal hole will fall away making it look much bigger than it really is. Often the trail running in and out gives a clearer idea of the width of the animal.

Atlantic grey seal trails in sand. (DW)

Above left: Mole trail just under the surface.

Above right: Otter entry into the water.

Well-used badger path.

Above left: Ephemeral roe deer trail through the grass.

Above right: Rabbit run.

Regular travel routes made by deer (known as racks) are often very obvious.

A roe ring created as the male roe deer follows the female, often forming a figure of eight around a tree.

Sometimes insects may leave a trail like these made by wood ants.

SCRAPES, DIGS AND COUCHES

This section looks at marks made on the ground by wildlife that doesn't fit neatly in any of the other categories. There is a crossover obviously, as a dig can become hole, but I have attempted to group the sign by behaviour and the majority of the sign described below relates to laying up/resting, feeding or scent marking, rather than house building. The thought process of what the animal was doing when determining what a piece of sign is becomes very important and runs throughout Part 2 of this book.

COUCHES AND BEDS

The most commonly encountered beds or couches in the UK are undoubtably deer beds, and they are characterised by a classic, flattened kidney bean shape. Depending on the substrate, they often show a bund, which forms against the animal's back as it lies down. Couches normally show significantly fewer hoof marks than scrapes, and the substrate looks decidedly flattened.

It has always been thought that, in leaf litter, roe deer will clear the ground to bed down and larger species won't. It is more accurate to think of this as a trend rather than an absolute. I have followed many deer over the years and their trails often lead to bedding areas. In my experience, larger species of deer, for example, fallow deer, often clear leaves away.

Size is a great giveaway in determining species, as is the presence of many same-age beds in close proximity. Red, sika and fallow deer are all herd animals. If multiple, same-aged beds are found, it is likely be one of these species.

Roe travel alone or in very small numbers, most twos and threes. They will come back to the same area, but the age of the beds helps distinguish this behaviour from many deer arriving to bed down at the same time.

In my experience, Chinese water deer and Reeves's muntjac do not clear leaf litter. The beds of the former are big enough to spot reasonably easily, but the latter takes some practice and are of a size where they could be confused with hare forms. Look for the bean shape and also hairs, which will occasionally be found (especially during moulting times) and can aid identification. In areas of grass and other herbaceous plants then no clearing is generally attempted, with deer preferring to just flatten areas to bed down.

As is often the case with tracking, there will also be times when the sign is not obvious. A deer may begin to clear the ground but not finish making something that looks like a scrape or may not lay down/stay long enough to flatten the area.

Although this is somewhat species dependent, deer will bed down temporarily to chew the cud, and these beds are often found surprisingly close to footpaths. The deer are usually long gone before dog walkers appear, and this can be a great point to think of when ageing trails, especially when considering how fresh the trail might be and whether it is worth following.

On other occasions, especially when people and dogs are at high density, deer will bed in some very tucked away and inaccessible places. Many times, I have followed fallow deer into areas where it is not at all obvious how they even got in, only to find them bedded there.

Deer will frequently bed on sloping ground, especially in areas where the terrain and aspect allow the scent of potential predators to rise up a slope. The territorial species, which are the larger, herd forming ones in the UK, frequently scat in their beds as they leave. I have never seen a roe deer scat in a bed it has just left, but I have found Reeves's muntjac scat in roe beds. Perhaps there is some weird psychological game going on between these species.

Deer also create areas of churned-up ground where they gather. This often happens if the tracker spooks them while trailing – having travelled off, after a certain distance they will stop, regroup and study their back trail. It is not the only reason for this behaviour, of course.

Left: A roe deer couch in the grass.

Below: Fallow deer typically do not clear the ground and may deposit scat as they get up to leave the bed.

The normal prepared bed of a roe deer. Note the bund of vegetation created by the animal's body.

Large areas of flattened earth, devoid of vegetation, caused by sheep shading themselves under trees.

A fallow deer gathering point. This is made more obvious due to the snow remaining everywhere the deer were not standing.

WILD BOAR NESTS

Wild boar will create quite elaborate nests or lairs with high walls of earth and may even line them with vegetation. This is especially true of sows when they give birth and their young are tiny. They do, in my experience, keep themselves to themselves, with the beds I have found being tucked away under trees and in dense thickets. Many characteristics in terms of flattening and hairs, as described for deer beds, also apply to wild boar.

Wild boar nest.

HARE FORMS

These can vary quite considerably in their clarity. Some are obvious, but others are so subtle as to be easily walked past. In a good example, it is possible to make out the position of the feet and head. Overall, hare forms tend to be rectangular in shape as opposed to the kidney bean shape of a small deer bed.

Above left: Brown hare form. The area indicated has been flattened by the rear feet of the animal.

Above right: Brown hare form in the buttress roots of a tree.

271

SCRAPES

SCENT MARKING

Many animals use their feet as a way of putting scent onto the ground, and some use their feet to distribute faeces and, I guess, some do a little of both. Classic marks in this category include deer scrapes, which in some species may also include wallows, and dog scrapes, which they do especially after defecation. Dogs will also bite and chew at the ground. Water voles paddle down their scat with their hind feet and then distribute their scent as they go about their business, while cats also scrape to bury their scat.

When looking for signs of otters under bridges, you may often come across little hills that have been scraped up from surrounding substrate or vegetation and then used by otters to spraint upon. In the absence of a high point for scent marking, they will create their own.

DEER SCRAPES

All our deer species potentially scrape and some regularly use the same areas over and over again. These scrapes are often located close to and on trails or other areas where deer congregate. They are not the shape of deer beds as described above and show no signs of flattening.

Roe deer scrapes, as described elsewhere in this book, may be accompanied by antler rubs on adjacent trees or just on their own. Timing is important as this activity is mostly carried out between April and July. To distinguish them from beds, look for all of the material scraped up in the same direction, and obvious hoof marks and grooves in the scrape. These scrapes are generally smaller and more rectangular than beds

Reeves's muntjacs also scrape and I have witnessed them scraping the ground, defecating in the scrape, and marking trees with scent from their pre-orbital glands. Their scrapes are usually close to a tree which may be used for scent marking and/or to protect the scrape from weathering. The ones I have found have, through repeated use, been quite large, in fact bigger than even a roe deer bed would be.

Above left: Domestic dog scrape after defecating.

Above right: Wild boar wallow. This may have been started by a red deer and then used by the boar.

Above left: This fallow deer scrape was associated with antler rubbing on low branch.

Above right: Reeves's muntjac scrape. Compare with the image of the roe deer bed (*see page 269*) for the lack of flattening.

BIRD SCRAPING

Birds scrape the ground regularly, especially game birds that behave like chickens. The size of the feet is a giveaway to the bird responsible. The finer the digit moving the earth, the finer the spoil. Characteristically, bird scrapes leave the soil looking like it has been raked. Blackbird scrapes can be found in urban settings as they forage for worms beside walls or on the pavement edge where soil and leaf litter accumulate. Birds will also collect mud for nests, which leaves a distinctive sign.

I once witnessed a buzzard scraping at the top of a mole hill, presumably in search of earthworms.

DIGS

SQUIRREL

Squirrel digs are identifiable by the bund of soil that often encircles the central hole. The base of a squirrel dig is quite small. Imagine it has placed an acorn or hazelnut in the bottom of the hole (which it frequently has). Alternatively, think of a squirrel's small nose and paws and imagine the size of hole it can actually make with this equipment.

Squirrel digs are most likely to be confused with the workings of a badger, which will use its powerful nose to excavate for invertebrates. The holes left by a badger usually have all the throw pushed up in the same direction. If badgers hunt for insects in vegetation they leave a characteristic spiral arrangement to the leaves or grass in what's known as a snuffle hole. It may be that in some snuffle holes the burrow of the unfortunate earthworm is also visible. When a badger is on a good run of finding invertebrates, they will turn leaf litter over to such an extent that it can look like miniature wild boar workings.

Far left: Pheasant scraping. Note the fine nature of the spoil.

Left: Buzzard excavating a mole hill.

Above left: Green woodpecker exploring an ant mound.

Above right: Beak marks from swallows collecting mud.

Above left: Grey squirrel dig, complete with acorn.

Above right: Grey squirrel dig showing the relative scale on the landscape.

BADGER

Badgers will dig with their claws to get at treats buried deeper down, like wasp grubs, and they will dig down quite a way to get at them. They will also break into ant hills looking for a meal. There are a couple things to look at to separate these digs from those of dogs and foxes.

Foxes, in particular, will dig to access the nests of small rodents. To aid identification, firstly think about the size of the debris coming out of a dig. This will depend greatly on the substrate, but we have very few mammals strong enough to move big rocks and large lumps of clay. Secondly, look at the width of the hole at the point where the spoil has been scraped towards the body of the animals. Dogs and foxes dig with their forepaws, pushing the spoil under their chest, which is a relatively narrow space. This is done in the same way as described for the fox earth in the section on holes. Badgers are wider and can also articulate their wrists and scrape out the sides of a dig, making it much wider. Scratch marks may also be visible on the sides of the dig walls. This is also true of other mustelids, and I have seen beech marten digs in mainland Europe marked in a similar way.

Badger nose dig, complete with worm hole.

Above left: Badger snuffle hole in grass.

Above right: This wasps' nest has been dug out by a badger. Note the amount of earth removed and spread far and wide, presumably very quickly.

Above left: Vole nest that has been dug out by a badger.

Above right: Red fox excavation of a vole nest.

Left: The narrow dig of a domestic dog.

Above left: Rabbit scrape with claw marks showing.

Above right: Rabbit scrape with scat just visible to the right of the frame

RABBIT

Rabbits also regularly make digs, which I believe are principally for scent marking. These are easily recognised as the throw mound is drawn up under the body, and they regularly deposit their scat on this mound. They are using glands under their chin and between their digits to scent mark these digs.

WILD BOAR

Wild boar are serious excavators of soil, and their activity is usually so deep and extensive that their digs are unlikely to be mistaken for anything else. Deer will often turn over leaf litter in search for acorns and chestnuts, but theirs is usually a much lighter touch, and therefore more likely to be confused with badger.

Below left and centre: Badger rooting.

Below right: Wild boar rooting.

DUST BATHS

Dust baths are used by a number of creatures, with birds being the most obvious. Their efforts are characterised by a bird-sized depression, often with a small bund of loose earth and perhaps feathers, or fragments of feathers, in and around the bath.

Rabbits and hares also dust bath. They will scrape up fine soil and therefore can often be identified by claw marks in the bath itself.

Above: Bird dust bath – in this case, a house sparrow.

Left: Rabbit dust bath.

PREDATION, CHEWS AND REMAINS

PREDATION

Everyone is eating something, and in some cases, they are eating each other. Sometimes kills can be difficult to interpret, and this is especially true if the mammal or bird is killed by one creature, and then the remains handled by another. Birds and mammals are killed by both mammals and birds. Providing the kill is fresh, it is relatively straightforward to decide which of these two groups of animals carried out the deed. What is often very tricky is narrowing down the predator to species level.

BIRD KILLS

Before investigating a bird kill, it is worth becoming familiar with the basic feather types as these are handled in different ways by mammals and birds.

PRIMARY FEATHERS

Primary feathers are responsible for forward propulsion and are located at the extreme end of the wings, attached to what is the equivalent of the human hand. They are usually pointed and also asymmetrical, in that there is more feather on one side of the central rachis (or quill) than the other. The thinner side is the leading edge, making it possible to identify which side of the bird it came from. The ends of the outer primaries may

Primary feathers.

also be emarginated, whereby they are cut away slightly on the leading edge, allowing the bird to adjust how the wind passes through its wingtips and therefore control movement and lift. Depending on species, there are usually ten primaries or sometimes twelve.

SECONDARY FEATHERS

Secondary feathers start close to the body of the bird and are attached to the equivalent of our forearm, and they are largely responsible for lift. They abut the tertiary feathers, which are closest to the bird's body. Compared with primaries, secondary feathers are shorter, rounded at the tip, usually have a curved rachis, and they are more symmetrical.

TAIL FEATHERS

Tail feathers, like the primaries, can be asymmetrical depending on their position in the tail. The central tail feather is symmetrical, and they progressively become more asymmetric towards the outside of the tail. As with primaries, this makes recognising the left and right side of the tail a fairly straightforward exercise. Typically, they are rounded at the tips, and the last few centimetres of the shaft as it enters the body are prominently curved. Some tail feathers are, however, highly modified. Woodpeckers, for example, have stiffened tail feathers which they rest on while climbing trees. Male pheasants have long tail streamers, which are used for communication and display.

Above: I have raised this blackbird secondary feather to illustrate the shape.

Below: This green woodpecker wing shows the secondary feathers closer to the body and the primaries out towards the tip.

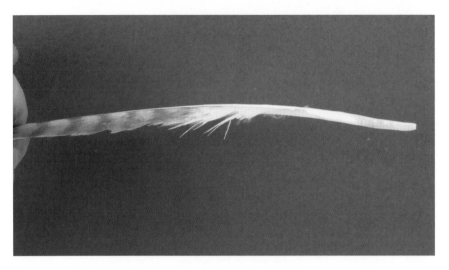

The 'kink' of a tail feather.

SMALL FEATHERS

All of the feathers mentioned above also have smaller versions covering the bare shafts of the bigger feathers. This is primarily to protect the photo-degradable shaft and rachis from sunlight. These are the coverts, and there are various groups of primary, secondary and tail coverts. The vast majority of bird feathers are contour feathers, which give the bird shape, keeping it waterproof and aerodynamic, and down feathers, which the bird uses for insulation.

Birds have many specialisations for feathers across different species. However, for our purposes in kill identification, we are mainly concerned with the arrangement made by the predator as the contour and down feathers are removed, and also the damage to and removal, or not, of primaries, secondaries and tail feathers.

This damage is often conclusive evidence in the 'CSI' of bird kills. However, keep in mind that sometimes when a bird is stressed (for example, by not having enough food) the feathers and quills may show these lean times as stress lines along which the feather can break or show wear that can be confused with predation. Also look at the base of the shaft as, in growing feathers (such as those of young birds or adults regrowing moulted feathers), these are filled with blood and often encased in a white sheath.

The first thing to think about when approaching a kill site is the arrangement of any plucked contour and down feathers. Birds killed by raptors tend to have their breast feathers plucked and scattered in the circle or semi-circle around the body being plucked.

You may find these smaller feathers pulled out in clumps, which may even have the flesh attached. This is typical for a mammalian predator.

Above left: Breast feathers plucked and scattered in a semi-circle around the body.

Above right: This woodpigeon has had its breast and head plucked by a hawk which was disturbed before it could eat properly.

 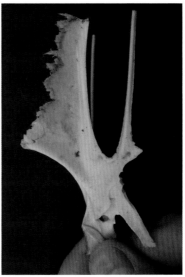

Above left: Classic 'bird killing a bird', with the head and breast meat taken.

Right: The notched sternum, characteristic of a bird of prey kill.

Clumped feathers pulled out by a mammal, in this case most likely a red fox.

Also check what part of the carcass has been opened. Birds of prey classically target the brains and the breast meat of their prey. They will also notch the keel of the sternum (or breastbone) with their bill as they clean the meat from this area. However, this is much more likely to be seen with a bigger bird of prey. Chunks of bone broken out of the sternum, in my experience, are generally caused by birds such as goshawks and buzzards. Sparrowhawks, particularly if they kill a big bird like a woodpigeon, don't really seem to notch the sternum. Presumably this is because their bills are not quite powerful enough to break the bones of a larger prey item.

With regards to sparrowhawks, there is, as with many birds of prey, sexual dimorphism in terms of size, with the females being significantly bigger than the males. This makes sense, as it means the smaller, more agile males can specialise in hunting smaller birds that the stronger but less manoeuvrable female may struggle to catch.

Woodpigeons are regularly killed by female sparrowhawks and they are probably at the limit of what these birds can handle. A fairly reliable sign when distinguishing the size of the killer, particularly on bigger birds, is if they have been moved or not. Birds such as goshawks and buzzards – in fact, all birds of prey – will often lift the victim up and take it to a plucking post, off the ground. This can be a tree stump, branch or any convenient mound in the landscape.

Although female sparrowhawks can kill woodpigeons, they are not strong enough to lift them far off the ground, so tend to eat them where they were killed. Another sign that a smaller raptor has killed at its limit are the signs of a struggle. I have a friend, Gavin Chambers, who surveys goshawks and explained to me that if a goshawk hits a woodpigeon, it is able to hold it still. The much smaller sparrowhawk is more likely to roll around and tussle with its victim, leaving trails of feathers and disturbance around the eventual kill site. I have used our Accipiters to illustrate this point, but the principles would serve with many other species of raptor. The size of the prey and the location it was eaten in can give you a clue as to the size of the animal killed it.

This plucking post is high off the ground, suggesting it was used by a large bird such as a goshawk.

Sparrowhawk plucking post on a moss-covered stump.

This is a feather from a young bird with the sheath and dark blood-filled shaft obvious. It has also been crushed by the teeth of a mammal.

The circular distribution of the feathers suggests this was killed by a bird, but the absence of the victim would point to a mammal moving it away.

Of course, a bird with plucked breast feathers, on a plucking post and with the breast meat gone are all fairly strong, if not conclusive, indicators of the work of a bird of prey. However, the sign is not always this clear. Sometimes, a bird of prey will kill another bird, and then have it scavenged by a mammal. It can be difficult to ascertain, for example, if the woodpigeon was killed by a bird and then scavenged by a fox, or if that fox killed the woodpigeon in the first place.

If a kill is small enough to be moved, mammal predators will move it and put it somewhere undercover or, in the case of foxes especially, cache it for later. I have successfully followed trails of feathers to the point where a fox has stored its food. If a big pile of feathers is found but no victim is left, a mammal has almost certainly moved it. Investigation may be necessary to discover if it was killed by that same animal or by a bird.

Bird carcasses that have been opened in areas other than the breast may also indicate the work of mammals. Domestic cats are often a culprit, especially on bigger species. Foxes and dogs will also crunch bones, and these can be found, together with the ends of feather shafts, in their scat. Several times, I have found the feet of woodpigeons inside fox scat. Cats tend to lick the carcasses clean and do not eat bone.

Above: The insides, foot and meat have been removed, which suggests a mammalian predator.

Left: The delicacy with which some of the meat has been removed suggests a bird of prey, but the crunched end of the thigh bone suggests a red fox.

FLIGHT AND TAIL FEATHERS

The flight and tail feathers can give us a clue that the victim has at least been handled by mammal. If a bird of prey eats the whole of its kill, frequently it will leave the primary feathers in place, taking all the flesh off the equivalent of our forearm. And to do this, it plucks the secondary feathers. It will also often leave the tail feathers alone.

Many sources suggest that birds of prey leave a beak-shaped crease at the base of the shaft where it enters the body of the bird. I have seen this, but it is much less common than you might expect. Feathers pulled out by a bird often show no real marks on them at all and can look just like naturally moulted ones.

How much is left of a kill can also help in identifying the predator. A woodpigeon probably weighs as much, if not more than a sparrowhawk, and I'm not sure if the sparrowhawk would be able to take off after eating the whole thing. Of course, many times, half-eaten carcasses are likely to be a result of disturbance.

Above left: The primary feathers are intact on this carcass, found under a buzzard nest.

Above right: This female sparrowhawk was predated, most likely by a goshawk.

291

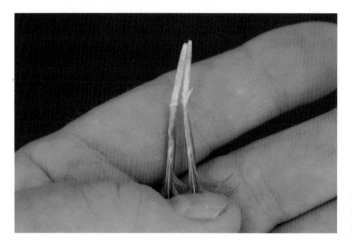

Feathers pinched by the beak of a bird of prey.

SHEARED FEATHERS

Feathers that have been removed by carnivores such as foxes, cats and the weasel family are often chewed close to the base of the shaft by the mammal's carnassial teeth. These are the shearing tools that all dog owners will be familiar with as the ones at the back of the jaw used to chew their favourite chew toy.

The angle that these feathers are sheared at can give a clue as to the size of the mammal carrying out the work. Animals such as foxes have quite a long length of shearing teeth at the back of their jaws and can therefore cut several feathers at one time. This leads to the angles of the cut shafts being equal and in line. Smaller mammals such as polecats and mink have correspondingly smaller jaws. They have to reposition their much smaller carnassial teeth as they work, leaving feathers with the ends sheared off at different angles. In both cases, these feathers are likely to be stuck together with the saliva of the animal feeding on them.

It is easy to be distracted by the pointy end of a feather and miss what's going on with the vanes themselves. Many mammals pull out feathers by grabbing them further up the quill away from the body. Breaks and holes in the feather's barbs, and kinks and holes in the shaft and quill itself, are frequently visible when this has happened.

Remember when looking at this, the potential for stress fractures, which could be confused with a feather being tugged and grabbed at.

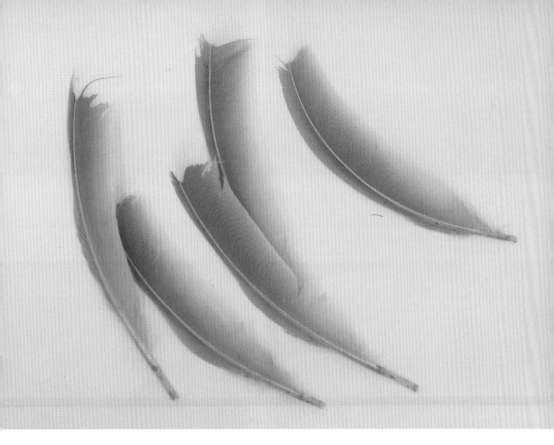

Above: Feathers pulled from the end by a red fox.

Below: Hen pheasant feathers sheared close to the end by the carnassial teeth of a red fox.

Above left: Tail feather pulled and broken by a domestic dog. Note the rounded end of this type of feather.

Above right: Blackbird killed by a domestic cat. (DC)

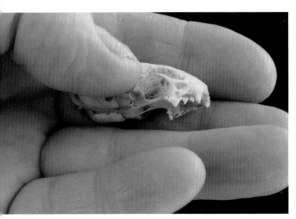
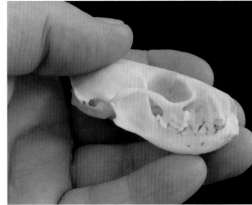

Size comparison of the carnassial teeth of various carnivores.

Above left: Weasel. *Above right:* American mink. *Below:* Red fox.

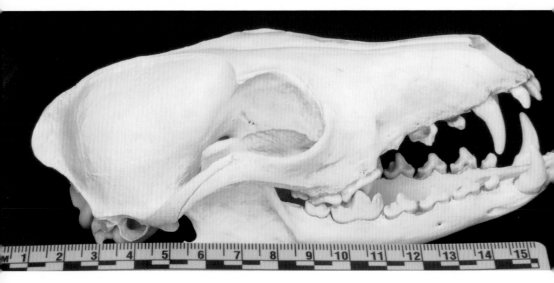

Red fox cache.

MOULTED FEATHERS

Naturally moulted feathers are generally found at specific times of year, and usually singly. Most species of birds need to keep flying, so they moult their flight feathers in pairs, one from one wing and the corresponding feather from the other wing at the same time. This is so they can maintain balance in flight. Water birds, particularly geese and ducks, will moult all their feathers in one go. They do this having finished breeding and go into something called eclipse plumage. If you're not aware of this behaviour, the resulting piles of feathers on the riverbanks or lake shores may lead you to think some dramatic bird-based carnage has occurred.

MAMMAL KILLS

Finding mammal prey in the UK is not as frequent as with birds. It could be that generally mammals are inconspicuous – a big pile of white down feathers is easier to spot than a dead rabbit.

Some of the same rules apply here, with birds of prey tending to pull out the fur of their victims and often taking them to a high point or post to do so. Mammal kills are scavenged by corvids, who often target the eyes. A small mammal killed by a raptor with the flesh entirely eaten may well look exactly like a bird treated the same way, with no broken bones and the carcass picked clean and often on a high spot.

Small rodents are frequently consumed whole, especially by birds of prey and larger animals such as foxes. Cats tend to eat most of the animal but leave a neat pile of intestines behind (for the cat owner to stand in). Small rodent kills are often hard to interpret when they are found.

The brains of animals are generally sought after by predators, and small rodents are sometimes found having been predated in this way. It can be difficult to tell who the predator is. Small mustelids are known to do this, and the yellow-necked mouse is known to eat the brains of torpid hazel dormice in nest boxes. This goes to show just how difficult it can be to be accurate when assessing predation.

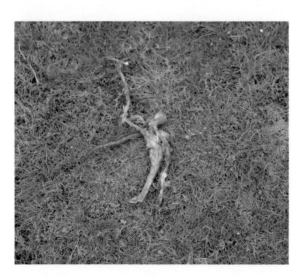

Brown rat that has been eaten by a buzzard.

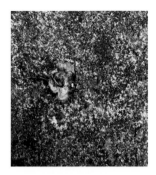 

Above left: This mouse was killed by a domestic cat. (DC)

Above right: Stoats and weasels often kill rodents with a bite to the neck. They also cache their kills and may sometimes drop them on the way to such a hiding place.

Rabbits are the targets of many predators, and some of these leave distinctive sign on their prey. Badgers are known to turn the skin inside out when removing it. They are also known to skin hedgehogs. Badgers will also dig out the nests of rodents and eat the young. Prey items killed by domestic cats and wildcats may also be taken to high points to be consumed.

Sheep worrying by dogs can be a big issue in the countryside and can lead to tales of 'big cats' abroad in our islands. Deer are also found killed in the countryside, and what follows is applicable to both.

Whether or not you believe in the tales of big cats, it is worth noting how cats kill prey in general terms, especially if the UK does eventually reintroduce the Eurasian lynx. Cats tend to ambush their prey with a short run or leap after stalking it. They fasten on with their claws and bite at the throat to suffocate the animal, or the back of the neck to kill it outright. Dogs tend to bite much more indiscriminately, targeting the back legs, belly, ears and throat of their victims.

If you need to be thorough with bigger mammal kills because of a lack of evidence, then skinning the animal may be the best way to be certain, as puncture wounds from a cat's canines can sometimes be found in the throat of the victim. The lynx may also break the vertebra of the neck in a struggle. I have found lynx kills in Poland and seen mountain lion kills in North America and they are very often dragged under cover. Dogs are unlikely to do this, or indeed even eat the animals they are chasing.

Above left: Rabbit kill, possibly by a domestic cat. (RB)

Above right: Rabbit fur that has been plucked out by a buzzard. (RB)

This brown rat has been killed and turned inside out by an otter. (RB)

This signal crayfish was killed by an otter. (DW)

Just the scales of this carp remain after an otter fed many weeks before.

The author examining a wolf kill in Poland. This red deer was targeted from the rear and gradually pulled down over a large distance.

Domestic dogs will often target the rear end of their prey just like wolves. (RH)

Domestic dogs often make multiple attacks on sheep, biting the head, neck and ears. (RH)

Lynx will also remove the hair and cover the body to cache it. Sometimes, they use fur of the prey to do so. A lynx will consume the carcass of a large animal over a few days and so needs to hide it from scavengers. Such scavengers include, in parts of their range, wild boar, wolves and brown bears.

Wolves enter the body of their prey frequently at the hind end and also disembowel it, and it could be that this is partly why our domesticated 'wolves' target these areas.

REPTILES AND AMPHIBIANS

Reptiles and amphibians are targeted by predators. The most common amphibian predation involves toads and frogs. Many animals eat them and some commonly leave remains.

Common toads are regularly skinned to avoid the poison glands on its skin. Polecats, badgers and otter are all known to this.

Raccoon dogs are also big consumers of amphibians, and several other species target both common frogs and common toads, eating the flesh and discarding both the eggs and the ovaries of the females. Polecats do this a lot at spawning time in early spring, as do buzzards. The discarded, hydrated egg mass, colourfully known as 'star snot', is often found on river and pond banks, and even in trees.

Above: This dead grass snake was found under a buzzard's nest.

Below: This frog was also found under a buzzard's nest.

Snakes are targeted by a number of birds. Buzzards commonly take snakes but so do pheasants, and this species is actually a serious threat to some of our reptiles. Pheasants will also dig out and eat the young of rodents, as will chickens. If you see them in action, you can see the resemblance to their dinosaur ancestors – and at the same time be pleased they aren't any bigger.

Above: Oviducts and spawn left behind after polecat predation.

Left: Frog spawn on a tree after buzzard predation. (DW)

SNAILS

A number of animals regularly target snails. Perhaps the most commonly known is the song thrush, which will find a convenient hard spot and use this as an anvil to break the shells of these creatures.

Rodents also target snails and characteristically break into the shell and gnaw down the spiral to access the flesh. Perhaps more unusually, you may also find snails placed in the workstation of a great spotted woodpecker (or perhaps a nuthatch) and opened like a nut.

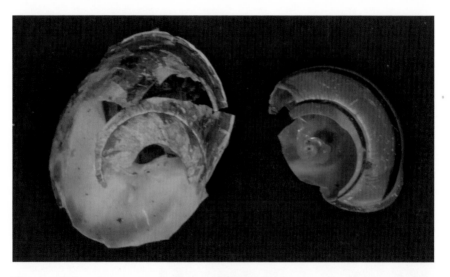

These snails have been eaten down the spiral by rodents.

Above left: Snail shell wedged into bark and opened, possibly by a great spotted woodpecker.

Above right: Song thrush anvil.

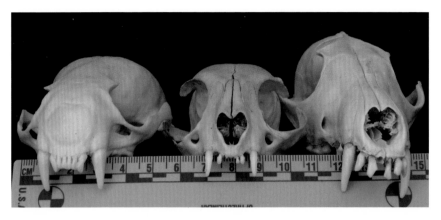

It is worth becoming familiar with the width between canines on common predators for both kills and in egg predation. *From left to right*: Otter (replica skull), domestic cat and red fox.

EGGS

Predation on eggs can be very difficult to interpret and here I offer some general rules to try to narrow down the likely culprits. Before trying to work this out, it is a good idea to become familiar with what a naturally hatched egg looks like.

A successfully hatched egg will be cut neatly by the egg tooth of the chick at the same height around its circumference towards the wider end of the egg. The edges are turned in and can be mistakenly judged to have been pushed in from the outside. This phenomenon is caused by the inner membrane of the egg drying and pulling the edge into the centre. You may commonly find both halves of the egg, with the smaller piece tucked inside the larger. The parent carries the egg fragments away from the nest so as not to alert a predator to the nest's presence. As an extra clue, there will be no blood or yolk in these two halves.

How and where a predated egg is opened can give a big clue as to who the culprit is. Small animals and relatively big eggs usually result in the eggs being opened from the ends. Mammals, such as mustelids, frequently open eggs from the side, creating a roughly rectangular-shaped entrance. Also, the puncture holes from the canines are often visible. The distance between the canines will give an idea of the predator.

Above: A naturally hatched egg with the top half tucked inside.

Below: Chicken eggs that have been opened by a captive red fox.

Above left: This pheasant egg has been handled by a red fox.

Above right: Chicken egg that has been opened by a hedgehog at the narrow end, together with smaller quail eggs opened by the same animal.

Small predators will push an egg around until it hits something hard and breaks. This makes the culprit very difficult to identify. A friend of mine, Rebecca Hosking, kept a rescued fox and at my request was kind enough to offer it some eggs and then describe how it opened them. The fox picked up the chicken egg, found a hard place in its enclosure, dropped the egg on it to crack it, and then rolled the egg over and entered through this weakened side.

Crows and their relatives are big consumers of eggs and often carry them off to a hard place to use as a kind of anvil and break into them from the side, creating a rectangular hole. This used to be my classic 'go-to' sign to identify bird predation on eggs. Then I began to write this book and started laying eggs out in the countryside and placing trail cameras next to them. I witnessed a magpie stabbing away at the chicken egg until it smashed it into so many fragments, I would have sworn it was the work of a rat or some other small mammal. I have seen rooks break eggs and then tip them up as if draining a bowl.

Canine holes visible on this egg with the second tooth hole partially hidden under a shell fragment.

I witnessed a rook eating this egg.

I had a trail camera on this egg, which was broken after several attempts by a magpie.

Pheasant egg opened by a corvid.

Sand lizard eggs.

Grass snake egg.

You can also be confused as a tracker by the eggs of reptiles. If we ignore terrapins, in the UK we have the grass snake and sand lizard that lay eggs, but unlike bird's eggs they are pliable and like thin plastic in texture.

REMAINS

Looking at the bits and pieces that are left after an animal has died or been killed is also a big part of tracking. However, skull and bone identification is a huge subject and very complex and deserves more attention than I can give it here. Identifying every bone on an animal to species level may not be possible in the field. However, it is worth getting familiar with the general shapes of the long bones from the legs of animals, as these are often distributed after predation and scavenging.

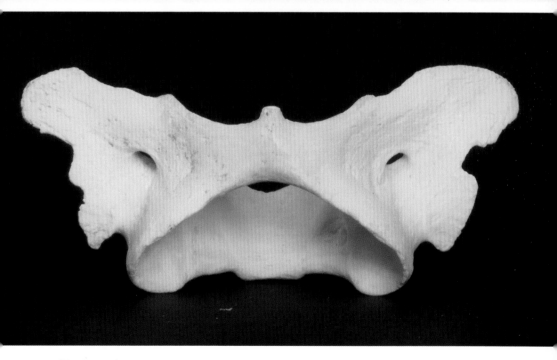

The butterfly-shaped atlas bone of a mammal, in this case a red fox.

The femur and the humerus are most likely to be confused as their general shapes are similar – look for the obvious neck that the ball of the femur sits on. The end of the humerus is much less defined, as it isn't actually socketed in the scapula.

I also like my students to be able to recognise the easily identified atlas bone on which the skull sits. The reason being that it often bears the marks of tools when an animal's head is removed and so can eliminate or confirm human involvement in the demise of a creature.

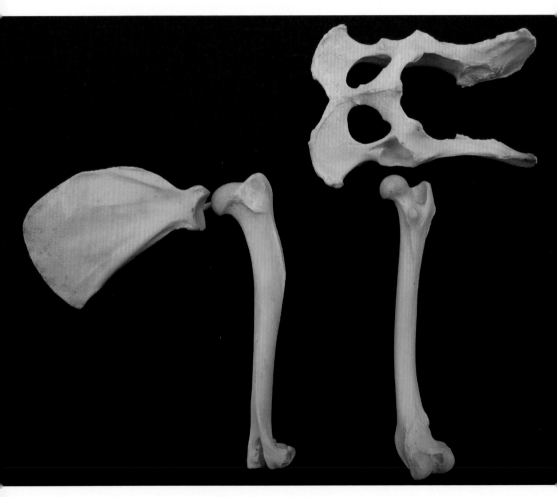

Humerus and scapula on the left and femur and pelvis on the right; both are from a red fox.

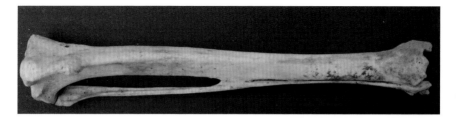

Tibia and fibula of a fox – note the sharp triangular leading edge of the thicker fibula.

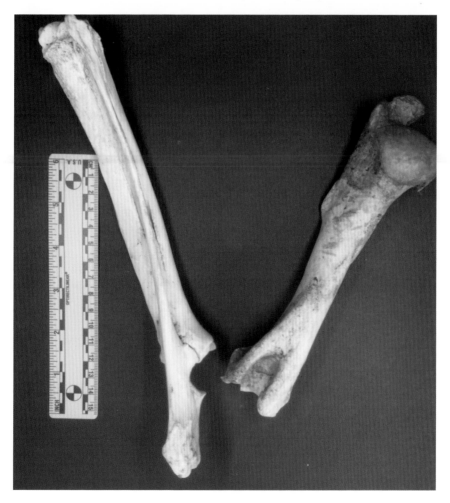

The humerus right and the radius and ulna of a fallow deer, note the elbow 'socket' in the thinner ulna that accepts the distal end of the humerus.

Sometimes animals will just be found dead and there will not be much of a clue as to what happened. I have found dead foxes and badgers outside their earths curled up as if asleep. Without doing a full post-mortem it can be difficult to be sure what happened. I do believe that often they get hit by cars but just make it home, or equally they could have been shot or poisoned. Sometimes, of course, they just die of natural causes and old age.

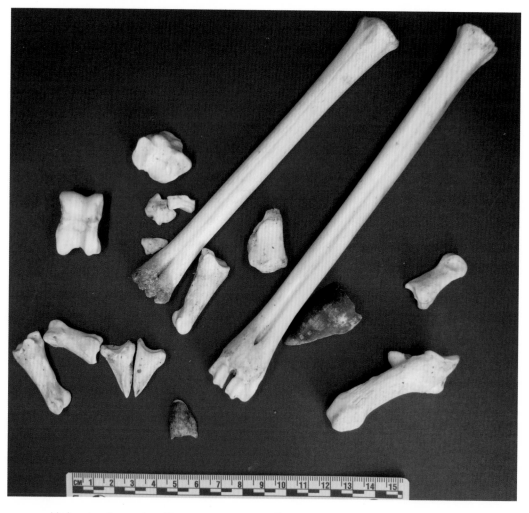

Various toe bones, hoof fragments , metacarpal/tarsal and cannon bones all found in the same area, I assume distributed by a red fox.

Above: Dead red fox just outside his burrow.

Left: This roe deer had severe tooth wear, indicating extreme old age.

SCRATCHES AND CHEWS

Many things seem to be worked by animals that leave telltale traces on them. For some, the reason is obvious. Rodents and deer, for example, will gnaw at bone, antler and even chalk to get at the calcium. However, keep in mind that the raking claws of badgers can leave marks on the debris they remove, especially lumps of chalk.

Badgers also create balls from wet earth that forms like a snowball as a result of their digging.

Sometimes, it is less obvious what's been happening or who's been involved. I have seen foxes play with tree guards, running with them, tossing them in the air and catching them like dogs.

Above left: Rodent teeth marks on chalk.

Above right: A badger has raked this chalk lump with its claws.

Above left: A badger ball.

Above right: A stick chewed by a domestic dog.

A tree guard that has been played with by a red fox.

REPTILE SLOUGHS

Reptiles regularly shed their skins, revealing a new and slightly bigger version underneath. These are very commonly found in early spring as they emerge from hibernation and it becomes something individuals do in a similar time frame. Lizards tend towards the fragmentation approach when getting rid of their old one. Snakes, however, can and often do take it off in one go and the remains are very similar to the real thing.

Adders have a characteristic pattern running down the centre of their spine which stays on the sloughed skin. Smooth snake scales do not have a central ridge, which is partly why they feel smooth in the hand. Grass snake scales have this central rib which always makes me think of a shield, although you may need a hand lens to see it. Slow worm sloughs are also frequently encountered and, to me, look metallic – if I squint, they remind me of chain mail.

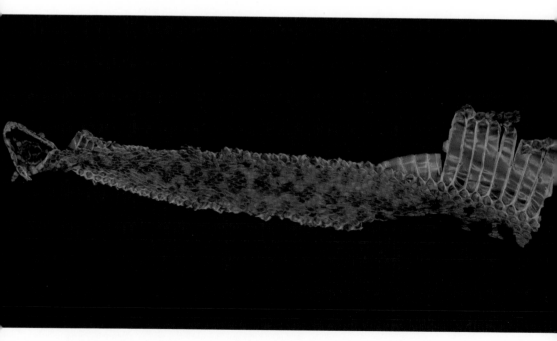

Adder slough showing the characteristic zig-zag pattern.

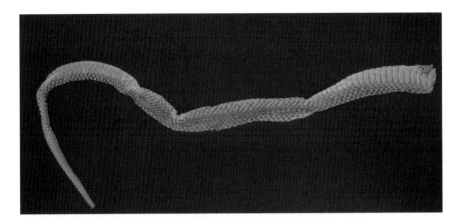

Smooth snake slough.

Above left: Slow Worm slough.

Right: Grass snake slough.

HAIR

Hair is another potentially huge subject and deserves more space devoted to it than I have here. It can often be found snagged on wire or in resting places. Most commonly encountered is badger hair, which is stiff and wiry, white at the base and doesn't roll between the fingers.

Deer hair is often found in beds and can help to identify these from scrapes. It is straight but hollow and so snaps easily.

Rabbit fur is fine and can be mistaken for down. It is often found in clumps as a result of fights and not predation.

Wild boar hair splits into a fork at the very end and is extremely wiry.

Animal hair, from left to right: red fox, rabbit, roe deer and badger.

SELECTED BIBLIOGRAPHY

Baker, N., *RSPB: The Nature Tracker Handbook* (London: Bloomsbury, 2019)

Bang, P., and Dahlstrom, P., *Collins Guide to Animal Tracks and Signs: the Tracks and Signs of British and European Mammals and Birds* (London: HarperCollins, 1982)

Brown, R., and Ferguson J. et al, *Tracks and Signs of The Birds of Britain and Europe* (London: Christopher Helm, 2003)

Elbroch, M. ,with MacFarland C., *Mammal Tracks and Sign: A Guide to North American Species* (USA: Stackpole Books, 2019)

Elbroch, M., *Bird Tracks and Sign: S Guide to North American Species* (USA: Stackpole Books, 2001)

Falkus, H., *Nature Detective* (London: Penguin, 1980)

Gooley, T., *Wild Signs and Star Paths* (London: Sceptre, 2008)

Harris, S., and Yalden, D., *Mammals of the British Isles: Handbook* (Mammal Society, 2008)

Moskowitz, D., *Wildlife of the Pacific North West* (London: Timber Press, 2010)

Nauta, R., and Pot, A., *Het Prentenboek* (Extra: Vledder, 2019)

Rhyder, J., *Animal Tracks Field Guide* (Woodcraft School, 2020)

GLOSSARY

Accipters: hawks specifically goshawks and sparrowhawks.

Carpal pad/s: wrist pads that support and protect the wrist.

Cyber (as in **Cyber Tracker**): refers to the data capturing software developed by Louis Liebenberg in South Africa – this doesn't form part of the evaluation process in Northern Europe.

Dew claw: digits that have changed position and/or function from the original mammalian foot. In the case of digitigrades, the thumb especially on the front foot is found high up the leg. In the case of ungulates, toes two and five are vestigial and sit behind toes three and four.

Digitigrade: an animal that stands or walks on its digits, finger walkers.

Distal: furthest away from the trunk of the body.

Half stride: the distance between the track of a specific foot and the track of the corresponding foot on the opposite side of the body. Left hind – right hind for example.

Hallux: toe number one, especially on a bird foot.

Interdigital pad: these are pads that protect the proximal end of toes and fingers, also called palm pads, intermediate pads, metacarpal pads (front) and metatarsal pads (rear).

Intergroup distance/space: the area between tracks on fast gaits where the animal doesn't contact the ground and therefore leaves no tracks.

Lagomorph: in the UK specifically rabbits and hares.

Latrine: place used for defecation regularly by an animal, often used for territorial marking.

Negative space: the area of a track that is not formed by pads.

Plantigrade: an animal standing or walking with its toes and palm pads flat to ground, sole walkers.

Primary feather: main flight feathers on the outer edge of a bird wing.

Proximal: nearer to the centre of the trunk.

Raptors: referring specifically to birds of prey but not owls.

Scat: excrement, also dung, droppings.

Secondary feather: these are placed on the 'arm' of the bird, closer to the body but adjacent to primary feathers, and are responsible for lift.

Sign tracking: identifying track and sign but not trailing.

Straddle: the width of the trail of the animal taken from the outer edge of the tracks on both side of the body.

Stride: the point where the track of a specific foot is seen to the point the same track is seen again.

Substrate: the medium that holds a track: sand, mud, snow etc.

Subunguis: the whole capping of the bony tip of a digit, here referring specifically to the part of a deer hoof that is not toe pad or unguis.

Toe pad: pad at the very end of the finger and toes, this is naked in most animals, including ungulates, and may show in the track. The exceptions are the lagomorphs, whose feet are covered in stiff hair.

Trailing: specifically using knowledge of the animal and its track and sign to follow and find wildlife.

Unguis: a nail claw or hoof, referring in this work specifically to the hoof and hoof wall of an ungulate.

Ungulate: referring to mammals having hooves.

Unguligrade: and animal that stands or walks on its hooves, nail walker.

Vestigial: a small remnant of something that was once greater or more noticeable.

INDEX